The Existence of God

Convincing and Converging Arguments

John J. Pasquini

UNIVERSITY PRESS OF AMERICA,® INC.

Lanham • Boulder • New York • Toronto • Plymouth, UK

Library of Congress Control Number: 2009934773
ISBN: 978-0-7618-4905-6 (paperback : alk. paper)
eISBN: 978-0-7618-4906-3

Cover photo by Fr. John J. Pasquini.

To Pope Benedict XVI

If any part or parts of this work are contrary to the teachings of the one, holy, catholic and apostolic Church, I reject that part or those parts as being a product of ignorance.

A special gratitude goes to the multitude of university professors whose time and suggestions made this project come to fruition.

Contents

Preface

Atheism has become a fad in our time. Young college students and the Hollywood crowd love calling themselves freethinkers, rationalists, and "brights." They love being part of what is popularly called the *New Atheism*. They carry around the works of Richard Dawkins, Daniel Dennett, Sam Harris, Christopher Hitchens and Michel Onfray like the sixties' generation used to carry around the works of the priest-scientist Teilhard de Chardin.

The following work is an affirmation of faith in God and a warning of the dangers of a world guided by the religion of atheism. It is a warning against a religion based on chance, deficient science, and deficient atheistic evolution (as opposed to theistic evolution).

The unhealthy state of atheism is increasing. For some it is a fad, for others it is possibly a personality disorder. Whether it is a fad or possible disorder, let us be prepared to save the lives of so many who are susceptible to atheism. We have enough lonely, empty, people in this world!

Introduction

There are essentially three types of atheists. One of the forms of atheism is called *categorical atheism*; this form of atheism is based on a reasoned, reflected inability to comprehend the possibility for the existence of God. It becomes *militant atheism* when this type of atheism is attached to a desire for converting God-believers. *Practical atheism* is a worldview where the question of God's existence is irrelevant to the meaning of life and the decisions of human existence: The belief or disbelief in God is irrelevant, for life, for such people, is lived out in a way that is indistinguishable from that of the categorical atheist.

Meaning is at the heart of the traditional proofs for the existence of God. The following three statements, understood in a broad sense, are at the heart of all the traditional proofs: 1) Nature is not able to establish its own sense of meaning; 2) Nature must somehow be meaningful; 3) Because nature must somehow be meaningful and because nature is not able to establish its own sense of meaning, then there is a need for a *Being* which can give meaning to nature.

The arguments that follow in this work are not meant to prove the existence of God in the same way that science proves a hypothesis. They are not proofs in the manner of the *natural sciences*. Rather, the *proofs* here must be seen as *converging and convincing arguments* that call one to question the plausibility for the existence of God. And when one studies the plausibility of the arguments one is left with the reality that the probability for God's existence is much more likely than his non-existence!

I

Filling the Emptiness

If God did not exist, it would be necessary to invent him.[1]

Voltaire

We were created for God, and thus when we deny God his place in our life, we end up empty and restless. Even the atheist Feuerbach had a lapse into logic when he stated: "Longing is the necessity of feeling, and feeling longs for a personal God."[2] It is for this reason that atheism is contrary to our intrinsic nature. It is for this reason that the debris of broken and despairing atheists litters the timeline of history!

We are born with an emptiness that seeks to be fulfilled. Many seek to fill this emptiness and sense of restlessness with power, fame, money, sex, drugs, and so forth. All these things can never fill the emptiness that is found at the core of one's being. Worldly *things* can never fill the barrenness of a soul searching for its creator.

A man buys his dream car and is filled with enthusiasm. At first he makes sure to park his car in a safe place and makes sure it is kept clean and running well. But as time goes by, what was once appealing loses it appeal. The scratch, the dirt, the very model of the car loses its attraction. Something nicer and newer attracts the eye. One abandons one's dream car, and seeks to buy the new dream car.

It is like a little child who plays with his brand new toy non-stop for the first week. After the first week the toy is nowhere to be found.

Those that seek fame and acquire it, find momentary satisfaction, but then they find fame empty. They thus seek to acquire more fame so as to recapture some sense of satisfaction.

Others seek wealth, and find momentary satisfaction, but then find themselves needing more. And the pattern goes on. It is an unending, destructive and empty cycle.

Only in God is there rest. Only in God do all of the world's goods find their proper place within a life of fulfillment, a life at peace with oneself and the world. When God fills the emptiness in one's life, then money, fame, chastity, and all the wonderful gifts that the world offers has its authentic preciousness. Study after study has shown that those who believe in a God have a happier and more satisfying life, including sexual satisfaction.[3]

It is on this basis that the famous seventeenth century mathematician and recognized genius, Blaise Pascal, could say that to believe in God is wiser than not believing in *him*. One who believes in God lives a happy life, and when one dies, one is rewarded with the gift of eternal bliss in heaven. If the believer ends up wrong, it is still a winning situation, for life on this earthly journey was one lived out in happiness and meaningfulness.

Because we were made for God, the real fundamental reality of the human person is his or her response to God. Since God is at the very core of the being, a person's innermost desire or longing cannot but be for God, and it is for this reason that those who deny God deny their very innermost reality or nature as a human person. It is for this reason that a person, no matter how he or she may try, can never eliminate the transcendental peculiarity of his or her being. God's self-communicating presence is at the very core of the person awaiting a response in freedom.

There is a *supernatural existential* factor innate to every human being, a factor which inevitably determines one's life. A *yes* to God moves one deeper into the mystery of self, the other, and God; a *no* response moves one away from this experience. One's choice, one's *yes* or *no* or indifference determines one's existence.

The human person has the ability to transcend himself or herself in openness into the reality of the self-communicating experience of God. Because of his or her inherent freedom, as a consequence of the supernatural existential factor, a person becomes so free that he or she has the capacity to take control of his or her own basic nature. A person is able to determine what he or she is and what he or she wants to be. At the heart of the definition of the person, therefore, is the ability for becoming. And this ability for *becoming* in *freedom* is the reason that one is open to that which is beyond: For it is this movement in freedom toward that which is beyond the self through self-causation, self-achievement, and self-becoming that the possibility for fulfillment is made possible. This fulfillment is found because this power to effect and enact oneself is at the very core of the meaning of the person, as a being meant for love.

The atheist, on the other hand,—continuing Pascal's thoughts—finds himself or herself in an awful predicament. He or she lives a miserable life on this earthly journey chasing after ghosts or gods of fame, power, drugs, and all forms of debauchery. Life becomes a slow debilitating journey into disintegration and death. And if the atheist does not let his or her desires rule, he or she simply becomes a leech on society's mores which he or she impulsively detests as restricting and stifling.

Is it any wonder that atheists have the highest suicide rate? Is it any wonder that atheists are acknowledged as being among the most unhappy, the most bitter, the most intolerant, the most aggressive, and the most likely to abuse drugs and alcohol? Catholic countries have a suicide rate of 4 percent per 100,000; Protestant Countries have a 13.8 percent rate per 100,000. Atheistic countries have a 31.1 percent rate per 100,000. Secular schools, at all levels, produce a higher rate of mental illness and mild forms of functional impairment. Atheists are half as likely to get married, twice as likely to divorce and are more likely to have few or no children.[4]

Atheistic intolerances, despair and frustrations are observable in atheistic regimes: from 1917 to 1969 the Soviets destroyed 41,000 of 48,000 churches. In Tibet 7,000 temples and monasteries were destroyed; in North Korea 440 of 500 Buddhist temples were demolished; and in Vietnam 240 of 700 Buddhist temples were dismantled. *Jane's Intelligence Review* of October 20, 2000 explains that 168 of 273 suicide bombings between 1980 and 2000 were not done by Muslims, but by Marxist atheists—i.e., the Liberation Tigers of Tamil Eelam being among the worst.[5]

Hitler, called by his Nazi contemporaries, the "greatest secularist of all time," was in fact a pagan trying to create a new Teutonic religion, after eliminating Judaism and Christianity. His new religion, highly influenced by the atheists Nietzsche and Schopenhauer, would be infected with the secular rage of the time, eugenics.[6] Jews paid a heavy, horrible price for an experiment in practical atheism!

Margaret Sanger, the Founder of Planned Parenthood, and in many ways the *mother of the culture of death* in America, embraced this new eugenics in the name of an atheistic utopian society.[7] The following are but a few of the many words she spewed:

- *"We don't want the word to get out that we want to exterminate the Negro population. . . ."*[8]
- *"Our failure to segregate morons who are increasing and multiplying . . . demonstrates our foolhardy and extravagant sentimentalism."*[9]
- *"Give dysgenic groups [people with bad genes] in our population their choice of segregation or compulsory sterilization."*[10]

- *"[There] should be more children from the fit, less from the unfit."*[11]
- *"Birth control must lead to a cleaner race."*[12]
- *"[Slavs, Latins, and Hebrews are] human weeds . . . a deadweight of human waste . . . eugenic sterilization is an urgent need."*[13]
- *"[Our objective is] unlimited sexual gratification without the burden of unwanted children . . . [Women must have the right] to live . . . to love . . . to be lazy . . . to be an unmarried mother . . . to create . . . to destroy. . . . The marriage bed is the most degenerate influence in the social order."*[14]

A society without God is open to the most barbaric of thoughts and acts. The words of Sam Harris and Richard Dawkins are woefully naïve in the face of Margaret Sanger: For Harris, "One of the enduring pathologies of human culture is the tendency to raise children to fear and demonize other human beings...[all in the name of God]."[15] For Richard Dawkins, "Without [a God-religion] there would be no labels by which to decide whom to oppress and whom to avenge."[16] (Margaret Sanger and the virulent words recorded in the texts of atheists simply contradict these words.)

Atheists, in their veneration of the self, as Feuerbach would put it, are unable to fill the void that only God can fill. Even Marx had to admit that there was something different about believers when he stated that religion was the opiate of the people. God truly does bring inner and outer peace. The fact that atheists have been trying to eradicate God and have failed miserably is a testament of this need for that which transcends oneself, God.

Pascal rightly pointed out the sad journey travelled by atheists. The dying words of famous militant and practical atheists say more about their lives than any explanation: Voltaire cried, "I have been abandoned by all. . . . I shall go into nothingness." Severus whispered, "I have been everything and everything is nothing!" Thomas Paine explained, "I would give worlds if I had them. . . . I am at the edge of hell all alone." Carlyle sniveled, "I am as good as without hope, a sad old man gazing into the final chasm." Sir Thomas Scott sobbed "Until this moment, I thought there was neither God nor hell . . ." Edward Gibbon despaired, "All is dark and doubtful." Sir Francis Newport cried, "All is over, all is lost." Hobbes said, "I am about to take a fearful leap into the dark. . . . " Marx shouted to his nurse, "Get out, get out. Let me die alone." Taleran admitted, "I am suffering the pangs of the damned." Vollney cried incessantly "My God, My God, My God . . ." Meravue exclaimed, "Give me opium that I may not think of eternity." Nietzsche, the most famous and influential atheist in history, spurted, "Blah, Blah, Blah . . . [the last words of an insane man]. Aldamont summarized it best, "Life was hell, and there is another hell ahead."[17] Yes, Aldamont, Pascal was right: only in God is our soul at rest!

NOTES

1. Voltaire, "Letter to the author of the three impostors," quoted in Thomas Williams, *Greater Than You Think* (New York: Faith Words, 2008).

2. *The Essence of Christianity*, trans. George Eliot (New York: Prometheus Books, 1989), 146.

3. Cf. www.psywww.com/psyrelig/happy.htm.

4. *American Journal of Psychiatry* 161, 2004: 2303-2308; World Health Organization, December 2005; *The Mental Health of Students in Higher Education*, Royal College of Psychiatrists, 2003; Aris Study, 2001. Much of the statistics in the following section are also found in Vox Day's *The Irrational Atheist* (Dallas: BenBella, 2008).

5. *Cox News Service*, April 25, 2004; Hayeem, "Destruction as Cultural Cleansing, Building Design," Feb. 3, 2006; *Asia News*. June 21, 2007.

6. Collimore, Papers Reveal Nazi Aim, 2002.

7. A detailed explication of Margaret Sanger's thoughts can be found in John Pasquini, *Pro-Life: Defending the Culture of Life against the Culture of Death* (New York: iUniverse, 2003), 1-4.

8. Letter to Dr. Clarence Gamble, Sophia Smith Collection, Smith College.

9. Margaret Sanger, *The Pivot of Civilization, The Cruelty of Charity*, Swarthmore College Library Edition, 116f.

10. Ibid., *Birth Control Review*, April 1932.

11. Ibid., vol. 3, no. 5, May 1919, 2.

12. Margaret Sanger, *Women, Morality, and Birth Control* (New York: New York Publishing, 1922), 12.

13. Ibid., *Birth Control Review*, April 1933.

14. Margaret Sanger, *The Woman Rebel*, vol. 1, n. 1, reprinted in *Woman in the New Race* (New York: Brentanos Publishers, 1922).

15. Sam Harris, *Letters to a Christian Nation* (New York: Alfred A. Knopf, 2006), 80. See also Harris, *The End of Faith* (New York: W.W. Norton & Company, 2004), 27, 29.

16. Richard Dawkins, *The God Delusion* (London: Bantam Press, 2006), 27. The argument that God-religions are divisive falls apart when confronted with these facts, *The God Delusion*, 259.

17. Cf. *The Sun Sentinel*, Fort Lauderdale Edition, 1968; cf. *Religion and Philosophy*, www.city-data.com/forum/religion-philosophy/330369-deathbed-admission-atheists.

II

Cardinal Newman's Argument from Conscience

Albert Camus wrote a book titled *The Fall*. It is a story about a successful Paris lawyer Jean Baptiste Clamence. He is an atheist, but a man of greatness and moral excellence.

In his career he never accepted a bribe or made any shady deals. He was always there to offer help, even at no expense, for the widow, the poor, the defenseless and the disenfranchised. He was the model citizen, the perfect model of integrity and dignity. In many ways he was a moral superman.

One evening while Jean Baptiste was coming home from work this would all change. It was late and Jean was returning home along the banks of the Seine River. While walking along the bridge Jean passed a young woman leaning over the railing of the bridge and looking intently into the water. Jean paused but continued walking. Suddenly he heard a splash and cries for help. The cries continued as the sound echoed downstream.

Jean paused and waited until the cries ceased. Then he slowly regained his strength and composure, and without looking back, continued walking home. He would tell no one what had happened.

The story ends with Jean spending the rest of his life in a world of homelessness, alcoholism, and debauchery. He spends his time looking back on that fateful night wishing he would have done something different. But it was now too late!

Jean recognized the reality of conscience.

Cardinal John Henry Newman explains the power of conscience as a convincing argument for God's existence:

If, as is the case, we feel responsibility, are ashamed, are frightened, at transgressing the voice of conscience, this implies that there is One to whom we are responsible, before whom we are ashamed, whose claims upon us we fear. If, on doing wrong, we feel the same tearful, brokenhearted sorrow which overwhelms us on hurting a mother; if, on doing right, we enjoy the same sunny serenity of mind, the same soothing, satisfactory delight which follows on our receiving praise from a father, we certainly have within us the image of some person, to whom our love and veneration looks, in whose smile we find happiness, for whom we yearn, toward whom we direct our pleadings, in whose anger we are troubled and waste away. These feelings in us are such as require for their exciting cause an intelligent being: we are not affectionate toward a stone, nor do we feel shame before a horse or a dog; we have no remorse or compunction on breaking mere human law; yet, so it is, conscience excites all these painful emotions, confusion, foreboding, self-communication, and on the other hand it sheds upon us a deep peace, a sense of security, a resignation, and a hope, which there is no sensible, no earthly object to elicit. The wicked flees when no one pursueth; Why does he flee? Whence his terror? Who is it that he sees in solitude, in darkness, in the hidden chambers of the heart? If the cause of these emotions does not belong to this visible world, the Object to which his perception is directed must be Supernatural and Divine; and thus the phenomena of Conscience, as a dictate, seeks to impress the imagination with the picture of a Supreme Governor, a Judge, holy, just, powerful, all-seeing, retributive, and is the creative principle of religion, as the Moral Sense is the principle of ethics.[1]

All cultures throughout the world and history have had a sense of right and wrong which cannot be explained by the simple learning of cultural mores, socialization or inculturation. It is this which John Henry Cardinal Newman knew so well.

Moral laws, like physical laws, are self-evident. What is moral produces harmony; what is immoral produces disunity and disintegration. When moral laws are followed, people prosper; when they are ignored, people suffer and often perish.

The following examples of sin and its consequences—which we can all relate to—should suffice to make the point. The sin of envy gives birth to hatred, slander, calumny, detraction, and joy at the misfortune of others. Anger leads to disputes, fits of passion, insults, blasphemy, rudeness, haughtiness and contempt. Vanity leads to disobedience, boasting, hypocrisy, unholy rivalry, discord, and stubbornness. Sloth (or acedia) gives rise to malice, rancor, discouragement, cowardliness, spiritual apathy or stagnation, forgetfulness of spiritual obligations, and the seeking after forbidden things. Avarice gives rise to disloyalty, treachery, fraud, deceit, perjury, harshness, hardness of heart, and an excessive desire for acquiring and maintaining things. Gluttony leads one to engage in improper jokes, coarse, loutish behavior, impurity, foolish conversation, and stupidity. Lust gives rise to spiritual blindness, poor judgment, impetuous or rash decisions, fickleness, instability, capriciousness, self-infatuation, and an inordinate attachment to this present life.[2]

Within every person there is an inner guide, judge, governor, or principle which helps one discern between that which is good—according to right reason—and that which is evil. This inner guide finds its origin in God and is called conscience. Our human experience may not recognize the origin of conscience, God, but it is aware of some internal pull tugging at the heart of its innermost being in regard to moral issues.

Atheists such as Nietzsche recognized conscience, but attributed it to mere human origins: "All credibility, all good conscience, all evidence of truth comes only through the senses."[3] "There are no moral phenomena at all, but only a moral interpretation of phenomena."[4]

Nietzsche could never adequately explain the common experience of right and wrong that has been experienced in all cultures and at all times.

To simply attribute conscience to cultural and/or biological evolution begs several questions: Where is the proof for this assertion, regarding cultural and/or bio-chemical evolution, if all cultures at all times have had a sense of right and wrong—thou shall not murder; thou shall not steal; thou shall not covet, etc. And if one assumes evolution, why do atheists find conscience so repressive? Conscience clearly evolved for the survival of the species—whether through a theistic or atheistic process. What is the psychological block that is preventing the person from accepting obedience to conscience?

Failure to inform and obey one's conscience has led to customs and practices that have been detrimental to the good of the species. Abortion, cloning, euthanasia, hybridization, contraception, promiscuity, and so forth are all detrimental to the species, and all related to the ignoring or repressing of conscience.

NOTES

1. John Henry Newman, *An Essay in Aid of A Grammar of Assent* (Westminster Classic, 1973), 109-110.

2. Cf. *Summa*, Ia IIae, q. 77, a.4f; q. 84, a.4.

3. Ibid, 278.

4. Walter Kaufmann, ed. and trans. *Basic Writings of Nietzsche* (New York: Random House, 1968), 275.

III

Ontological Argument Revisited

Anselm's ontological argument for the existence of God has been one that has received a great deal of debate over the centuries. It was rejected by philosopher-theologians like Gaunilo and Aquinas. Attempts were made to resuscitate the argument by Descartes, but this attempt was futile in the face of Kant's criticisms.

The 1960's, however, brought about a new examination of the argument. Philosophers such as Charles Hartshorne have pointed out a significant flaw in the past evaluations of the ontological argument: As he explains, "[the philosophers of the past] failed to see that Anselm presented two forms of . . . [his ontological argument], the second involving a genuine conceptual breakthrough."[1] The criticisms of the ontological argument (in the past) had always focused on the first argument, failing to take into account the second argument. The second version of the ontological argument by-passes all the criticism thrown at the first. Thus the revival.

The following is my personal explication, influenced by Norman Malcolm, of the second ontological argument:[2]

1. God is as a matter of definition a perfect being.
2. The existence of a perfect being is either a reality or logically impossible.
3. The existence of a perfect being is not logically impossible.
4. If a perfect being is logically possible as a reality, then the existence of God is favored over his non-existence.

While the idea of a unicorn or flying cow is not a logical possibility in reality, the idea of God is! This argument takes the ontological argument out of the sphere of *ideas* and into the realm of the empirical.

NOTES

1. *Anselm's Discovery: A Re-Examination of the Ontological Proof for God's Existence* (Chicago: Open Court, 1991), back cover.
2. Cf. www.iep.utm.educ/o/ont-arg.; Norman Malcolm, "Anselm's Ontological Argument," *Philosophical Review*, vol. 69, no. 1 (1960), 41–62).

IV

St. Thomas Aquinas: The Five Ways[1]

The first and most obvious way [to prove the existence of God] is based on change. We see things changing. Anything that changes is being changed by something else. . . . This something else, if itself changing, is being changed by yet another thing; and this last change by another. Now we must stop somewhere, otherwise there will be no first cause of the change, and, as a result, no subsequent causes. (Only when acted upon by a first cause do intermediate causes produce a change . . .) We arrive then at some first cause of change not itself being changed by anything, and this is what everybody understands by God.

The second way is based on the very notion of cause. In the observable world causes derive their causality from other causes; we never observe, nor ever could, something causing itself, for this would mean it preceded itself, and this is not possible. But the deriving of causality must stop somewhere; for in the series of causes an earlier member causes an intermediate and the intermediate a last (whether the intermediate be one or many). Now eliminate a cause and you also eliminate its effects: you cannot have a last cause, nor an intermediate one, unless you have a first. Given no stop in the series of causes, no first cause, there will be no intermediate causes and no last effect; which contradicts observation. So one is forced to suppose some first cause, to which everyone gives the name of God.

Intelligent design which we will discuss later is a powerful affirmation of Aquinas' first two proofs—as are the very laws of nature.

The third way is based on what need not be and on what must be. . . . Some of the things we come across can be but need not be, for we find them springing up and dying away, thus sometimes in being sometimes not. Now everything cannot be like this, for a thing that need not be, once was not; and if everything need not be, once upon a time there was nothing. But if that were true there would be nothing even now, because something that does not exist can only be brought into being by something already existing. If nothing was in being nothing could be brought into being, and nothing would be in being now, which contradicts observation. Not everything therefore is the sort of thing that needs not be; some things must be, and these may or may not owe this necessity to something else. But just as a series of causes must have a stop, so also a series of things which must be. One is forced to suppose something which must be, and owes this to nothing outside itself; indeed it itself is the cause that other things must be. This is God.

SUBSISTENT EXISTENCE AND THE THIRD WAY

What keeps you and me from popping out of existence? What keeps anything from just popping out of existence? In scientific terms, what keeps matter from ceasing to exist?

Elementary particles make up matter. Matter is made up of chemicals, and chemicals are made up of molecules, and molecules are made up of atoms, and atoms are made up of protons, electrons, neutrons, and quarks. When we get to the smallest elementary particle in the universe, the question still arises: What keeps it from popping out of existence? Either this foundational particle *always existed* as the building block of all existing things, or God, *as existence itself*, is the source and sustainer of all that exists.

Human experience shows us that there is nothing in life that exists that did not have something to put it into existence. God, on the other hand, is *subsistent existence*; he is *existence itself. He does not come into existence, for he is existence.*

What is more plausible: the existence of an eternal particle "X" or the existence of an eternal reality we call *subsistent existence, existence in itself,* God? Probabilities favor God!

The fourth way is based on the gradation observed in things. Some things are better, truer, more excellent than others. Such comparative terms describe varying degrees of approximation to a superlative. . . . Something therefore is the truest and best and most excellent of things, and hence the most fully in being. . . . Now when many things possess some property in common, the one most fully possessing it causes it in the others. . . . Something therefore causes in all other things their being, their goodness, and whatever other perfection they have. And this is what we call God.[2]

St. Anselm in the *Monologion* echoes St. Thomas' argument. The argument can be summarized in the following way:

(1) Men desire objects they think to be good—objects that vary in degree of goodness. (2) Because the variance in degree is intelligible, there must exist an invariable principle of order, i.e., a supreme good that is the source of all goodness. (3) The objects of desire have natures that vary in worth and dignity. (4) Because the worth of natures varies in degree there must exist a supreme nature that is invariable and does not admit comparison, i.e., a self-subsistent nature that is the originative principle of all variable natures.[3]

In other words, how do you know what is good unless you can distinguish between good and evil? How do you know what is better than another, unless one has the ability to assess good or better within a gradation from good to evil or evil to good. If there is such a gradation, then there must be an ultimate good, *good in itself*, God.

God is not simply good; he is goodness itself.

The fifth way is based on the guidedness of nature. Goal-directed behavior is observed in all bodies obeying natural laws, even when they lack awareness. Their behavior hardly ever varies and practically always turns out well, showing that they truly tend to goals and do not merely hit them by accident. But nothing lacking awareness can tend to a goal except it be directed by someone with awareness and understanding. . . . Everything in nature, therefore, is directed to its goal by someone with understanding, and this we call God.[4]

David Conway's philosophical and scientific work on the origins of life explains Aquinas' *fifth way* in modern terms:

[After one can overcome the challenge of how to produce life from non-life, living matter from non-living matter, then one must explain the problem of the teleological nature to life.] In being alive, living matter possesses a teleological organization that is wholly absent from everything that preceded it. . . . [How do we explain] the emergence, from the very earliest life-forms which were incapable of reproducing themselves, of life-forms with a capacity for reproducing themselves? Without the existence of such a capacity, it would not have been possible for different species to emerge through random mutation and natural selection. Accordingly, such mechanism cannot be invoked in any explanation of how life-forms with this capacity first 'evolved' from those that lacked it." [These biological phenomena] provide us with reason for doubting that it is possible to account for existent life-forms in purely materialistic terms and without recourse to design.[5]

Or as the Nobel Prize winning physiologist George Wald explains:

How is it that, with so many other apparent options, we are in a universe that possesses just that particular nexus of properties that breeds life? It has occurred to me lately—I must confess with some shock at first to my scientific sensibilities—that both questions might be brought into some degree of congruence. This is with the assumption that mind, rather than emerging as a late outgrowth in the evolution of life, has existed always as the matrix, the source and condition of physical reality—that the stuff of which physical reality is constructed is mind-stuff. It is a mind that has composed a physical universe that breeds life, and so eventually evolves creatures that know and create: science, art, and technology-making creatures.[6]

The *guidedness* of nature or the goal-directed, end-directed, self-replicating directed nature of life-structures is more a product of an intelligent designer, God, than chance. Life could not have evolved the way it has without direction from a director! Evolution is much more a "converging and convincing" argument for God's existence than his non-existence!

The key points to Aquinas' above arguments are as follows: There is observable and obvious change in the world and it is obvious and observable that this change requires something or someone to cause it. There is an obvious and observable order in the world (there would be no science if this were not so) and this order requires someone or something to put it into order.

These points lead to essentially the following questions: Do things that change always have a cause for the change? Do causes of things cause other things to change? Do things that are in order have someone or something to put them in order? What does our experience teach us?

Experience teaches us that everything that changes or has intermediate causes or has order has someone or something to have brought about this change, this cause, this order. Probability favors God since our understanding of change, cause, and order is in accord with our experience of life. Human experience teaches us that it is more likely that *things* have a beginning, for all we know in life is marked by beginnings. We call this beginning without a beginning, the source of all beginning, the first cause, the prime mover, the source of all order, *existence itself, subsistent existence*, God. (God is not in existence as much as he is *existence itself, subsistent existence*.) God is not simply a cause; he is cause itself. He is not simply a change: he is change itself. He is not simply a divine orderer: he is order itself. God is not simply something that exists: he is existence itself.

Aquinas' fourth and fifth arguments follow the same pattern. God is not simply perfect: he is perfection itself. God is not simply beautiful: he is beauty itself. He is not simply good: he is goodness itself. He is not simply true: he is truth itself.

Aquinas' arguments are fundamental for the understanding of the *Intelligent Design* arguments favoring the existence of God.

NOTES

1. For the *New Atheists* Aquinas is very problematic, and it is for that reason they seem to avoid him at all costs, or to simply breeze over the proofs with little critical thinking, as is the case with Richard Dawkins in *The God Delusion*, 77, when he states: "[Aquinas makes] the entirely unwanted assumption that God himself is immune to regress." Dawkins sadly shows his ignorance of what is meant by "an infinite regress." He clearly exemplifies Einstein's assertion that scientist are poor philosophers.

2. Thomas Aquinas, *Summa Theologiae: A Concise Translation*, ed. and trans. Timothy McDermott (Westminister: Christian Classics, 1989), 12–14.

3. *Catholic Encyclopedia*, 700.

4. *Summa Theologiae: A Concise Translation*, 12–14.

5. David Conway, *The Rediscovery of Wisdom* (London: Macmillan, 2000), 125, quoted in Antony Flew, *There is A God: How the World's Most Notorious Atheist Changed His Mind* (New York: HarperOne, 2007), 88.

6. George Wald, "Life and Mind in the Universe," in *Cosmos Bios, Theos*, ed. Henry Margeneau (LaSalle: Open Court, 1992), 218.

V

Intelligent Design

Intelligent design argues quite simply that the evidence of science favors design and necessity over chance and necessity. Intelligent design is, from my perspective, *not a science* but a proof in the Catholic sense, a "convincing and convergent" argument favoring God's existence rather than his nonexistence.

Intelligent design comes in a variety of forms. The form that I will follow incorporates micro and macroevolution.[1]

Intelligent design argues that "intelligent causes are necessary to explain the information rich structures of biology and that these causes are empirically detectable." It argues for a finely tuned universe that can only be explained by design.[2]

Design and necessity rather than chance and/or necessity are more probable an explanation for our world. The universe is not a chaotic series of bodies. Quite the contrary, the universe is so finely tuned that the probability of its existence is mathematically implausible without a divine designer.

In the nineteenth century, design in creation became less popular, as did the relationship between spirituality and psychology. By the latter part of the twentieth century, a new advent in psychology reintroduced the importance of spirituality into the field of psychology; likewise, due to developments in the sciences of physics, cosmology, and molecular biology a new advent in intelligent design came to the fore once again. Britain's legendary atheist, Antony Flew, became a theist—a believer in God—with this new advent:[3]

> It now seems to me that the findings of more than fifty years of DNA research have provided materials for a new and enormously powerful argument for design.[4] [This is] the world picture, as I see it, that has emerged from modern

science.[5] *The enormous complexity [of DNA] . . .looks to me like the work of intelligence. . . .*[6]

The world renowned molecular biologist Michael Denton explains this revolutionary development caused by advances in molecular biology: "The complexity of the simplest known type of cell is so great that it is impossible to accept that such an object could have been thrown together suddenly by some kind of freakish, vastly improbable, event. Such an occurrence would be indistinguishable from a miracle."[7]

Even atheists have had trouble dealing with the obvious appearance of design in nature: Richard Dawkins, the new but less philosophically astute Antony Flew, remarks: "Biology is the study of complicated things that give the appearance of having been designed for a purpose."[8] His book *The Blind Watchmaker* is an attempt to explain away this sense of design. The atheist biologist Francis Crick, the co-discoverer of the DNA Double Helix, likewise reluctantly forewarned his colleagues: "Biologists must constantly keep in mind that what they see was not designed, but rather, evolved."[9]

Atheists find themselves having to fight off what they see in order to fulfill what they desire—a godless world.

Chance has no intelligence, no choice, no causal power, yet we are expected to believe that a finely tuned, ordered being, called a human being, is the simple production of a chance association of matter and bio-chemical forces.[10] We are expected to think that our universe, with all its laws and order, is simply a reality devoid of design.

BIOLOGICAL DESIGN

The cell is that which reads DNA and translates it into the structures necessary for life. Can evolution without God explain the birth of the cell?

The odds of a cell developing by chance, the odds of DNA developing by chance, the odds of a cell cooperating with DNA by chance, is impossible to fathom?[11] Scientists have pointed out that the odds of a DNA strain arising by chance is a statistical impossibility (1.6 followed by 59 zeros to one). The existence of the human cell being formed randomly some 3.7 billion years ago is statistically impossible.

Alternative explanations are needed. The famous and legendary scientist Francis Crick, the atheist co-discoverer of the structure of DNA, had trouble dealing with the statistics involved with the birth of the cell and human life in so short a time period (3.7 billion years). It is for this reason that he proposed what has become known as the *panspermia thesis* which argues that intelligent aliens seeded the earth with life. Even Crick had to concede to an intelligent cause or being for life on earth. But, I ask, "Who created these aliens?"

Others have been less extreme and have argued that meteors impregnated with the seeds of life brought life to earth.

It is also for this reason that many scientists hold by faith (as does Richard Dawkins)—since there is not a single shred of evidence for its support—that there are billions upon billions of planets or billions of billions of universes.[12] By proposing *multi-world* or *multi-universe* theories, the mathematical probabilities for the world as we know it becomes smaller and more probable. Secular scientists confronted by intelligent design theorists often are left with simply saying: "Well, we are here, so it must have happened somehow, someway."[13]

Catholics believe in faith seeking understanding, and knowledge nourishing faith. The *panspermia thesis* or the *multi-world, multi-universe theories,* in whatever form, are examples of blind faith! It is not faith seeking understanding nor is it knowledge seeking to nourish faith—or the advancement of further knowledge. In the words of the philosopher of science, Swinburne, "It is crazy to postulate a trillion (causally unconnected) universes to explain the features of one universe, when postulating one entity (God) will do the job."[14] Or as Antony Flew explains: "[Multi-universe] or not, we still have to come to terms with the origin of the laws of nature, and the only viable explanation here is the divine Mind."[15]

The scientific principle of simplicity (*simplex sigillum veri*) which states that the simplest explanation of phenomena is the most probable is contradicted by the *panspermia* and the *multi-world, multi-universe* theories.

The earth is a privileged planet, a planet where life, and complex life at that, exists. One would expect that in a universe as expansive as ours that life would be abundant, yet even a single cell cannot be found anywhere except on this privileged planet. What are the odds? You would expect the universe to be teeming with life—thus, the Viking mission's disappointment.

All that we experience is either a product of chance or of design. The evidence, common sense, and logic favors design. And God is the designer. *Simplex sigillum veri.*

TIGHT FUNCTIONAL INTEGRITY AND COMPLEXITY

[When] we come to inspect the watch, we perceive . . . that its several parts are framed and put together for a purpose, e.g. that they are so formed and adjusted as to produce motion, and that motion so regulated as to point out the hour of the day; that, if the several parts had been differently shaped from what they are, of a different size from what they are, or placed after any other manner, or in any other order, than that in which they are placed, either no motion at

all would have been carried on in the machine, or none which would have answered the use, that is now served by it.

There cannot be design without a designer, contrivance without a contriver, order without [an orderer]; and relation to purpose, without that which could intend a purpose; means suitable to an end, and executing their office in accomplishing that end, without the end having been contemplated, or the means accommodated to it. Arrangement, disposition of parts, subserviency of means to an end, relation of instruments to a use, imply the presence of intelligence and mind.

The inference . . . is inevitable. [The] watch must have had a maker; that there must have existed, at some time and at some place or other, an artificer . . . who formed it for the purpose which we find it actually to answer; who comprehend its construction, and designed its use. [16]

William Paley

As mentioned earlier, the cell is that which reads DNA and translates it into the structures necessary for life. But why does it read this DNA and why does it translate it into structures? What gives it its dynamism? Why must it be anything other than a pile of chemicals and forces just sitting there or moving around aimlessly? What gives it its drive, its purpose, its end? What makes a cell, building material, ordered by a blueprint, DNA, to build? Is the answer found in chance or in design?

Design is favored over blind chance, and design implies a designer, God!

The human eye is another example where design is favored over chance. Light is absorbed by a molecule in a human eye. The molecule in turn changes the attached protein, which in turn begins a cascade of precisely integrated events or reactions at the molecular level. From this intricate process a nerve impulse is triggered and is transmitted in such a manner that sight becomes the eventual end of the cascade. Eliminate any one of the parts or processes that makes sight possible, and there would be no sight.

Either one has to accept some form of chance, simultaneous evolution of structures or one has to accept a divine providential guider of evolution. The chances of a series of useless and unnecessary parts coming together simultaneously and producing sight through chance and blind or random natural selection is implausible.

To accept blind evolution or chance evolution is to accept that all these complex components hung around until all the necessary chance mutations and all the necessary natural selection processes could interact in such a simultaneous fashion as to produce sight.

This is similar to a human being walking around with a large wing-like floppy ear, hoping that one day he or she would have the gift of flight. One would have to hang around hoping that this floppy ear would not be detrimental to survival and to being selected out of existence. Then one would have to hope that this mutation is passed on, and then one would have to wait around with the hope that another ear would become equally large, equally wing-like and floppy, then one would have to hang around for the brain to be so reconstructed by mutations so as to allow for the ability to make these humongous floppy ears flap properly. Flight would be a great advantage to survival. But what are the odds? And as with the case of the eye, if any one of the parts is removed without a comparable replacement, the system breaks down.

It is like acquiring, without your knowledge and desire, a set of car wheels through UPS. The next day comes, to your surprise, a car body. Then the next day an engine, and then a transmission, and then several other parts arrive. Despite all these wonderful gifts, you still do not have a car. You just have parts. An intelligent car designer is necessary to put all these parts together in order to have a functioning car. Now who would manufacture tires unless they knew what they would be used for? Who would construct an engine unless they knew what it would be used for? In and of themselves, these things are useless. Only when they are organized or ordered in such an intelligent way, can one have that which we call a car.

Only a divine design could plan out the creation of the parts of the eyes—which are useless in and of themselves—in such a fashion that they become present in a cohesive manner and become interactive. The eye is an example of *tight functional integrity.*

The irreducible complexity of some systems can only be explained by a God-guided evolution. The biochemist Michael Behe explains, "An irreducibly complex system cannot be produced directly . . . by slight, successive modifications of a precursor system, because any precursor to an irreducibly complex system that is missing a part is by definition nonfunctional. . . . Since natural selection can only choose systems that are already working, then if a biological system cannot be produced gradually it would have to arise as an integrated unit, in one fell swoop, for natural selection to have anything to act on."[17]

While Behe's statement neither affirms nor denies evolution or God, I do. I assert, if evolution is true, it is only so because evolution favors God's providential guidance and intervention rather than blind chance. The odds of a Chihuahua singing opera is more likely than random chance producing a cell or an eye. Without the existence of God, evolution cannot be sustained as a viable theory.

But if God is necessary for evolution, why are things imperfect. How do we explain poor eyesight or flaws in human structures? Why would the intelligent designer not produce a perfect eye, for example? One reason is tied to the theological teaching on original sin. But this is a matter a faith—albeit confirmed by reality. The second is simply the fact that we are still evolving? The end product being perfection!

INDIRECT EVOLUTION

What about the idea of *indirect evolution* as a solution to the problem of independent parts coming together to operate as a system. That is, cannot parts that function in another bodily system be used with newer parts—that is *co-opted*—to develop a new system, a system like the eye. In other words, cannot parts that are performing functions in separate systems become integrated into new systems, when new parts evolve into existence?

When we examine the intracellular transport system, blood clots, the immune system, DNA replication, electron transport, telomere synthesis, photosynthesis, transcription regulation, etc., we are convinced that these systems could never have evolved from precursors or from co-opting pre-existing systems. When we examine cilium, bacterial flagellium, carnivorous plants, the water vascular system of starfishes, the reproduction system of fleas, the respiratory system of birds, mammalian hearts, the pollination mechanism of the orchid, the metamorphosis of butterflies, the amniotic system of reptiles, the structure of feathers, and the complexity of the life cycle of the liver fluke we are convinced that these complex systems could not have evolved by co-opting previously existing systems. They are far too complex and tightly integrated. The universe is not old enough to account for the existence of these systems.

Michael Denton gives the example of the whale to make the same point:

> [In order to transform a land mammal into a whale the following would be needed]—forelimb modifications, the evolution of tail flukes, the streamlining, reduction of hind limbs, modifications of skull to bring nostrils to the top of the head, modification of trachea, modifications of behavior patterns, specialized nipples so that the young could feed underwater. . . . One is inclined to think in terms of possibly hundreds, even thousands of transitional species on the most direct path between a hypothetical land ancestor and the common ancestor of modern whales.[18]

The co-opting of previous systems cannot explain the complex development of organisms.

This again shows that evolution is more likely the product of an intelligent designer than chance.

Furthermore, if co-opting were as common as it would have to be to explain most biological systems, we would expect all species to be crammed with an abundance of vestigial parts. The body would have vestiges of all kinds of useless bio-chemical debris. You would expect the body to be overflowing with failures of evolution that natural selection could not get rid of. This is not the case!

Some like to point out that humans do in fact have worthless vestigial parts (i.e., tonsils, adenoids, an appendix, a coccyx—tailbone). Recent studies, however, have shown this not to be the case. Once these parts were thought of as simply vestigial leftovers, but advancements in science show the opposite; the coccyx or tailbone is essential for connecting the muscles to the pelvis and the tonsils, adenoids, and the appendix are important parts of the human immune system.

Evolution here favors God not blind chance.

Even if there were vestigial structures left over, that in no way denies the divine. For Darwin, all things are evolving toward the *utopian man*. For the Christian, all things are evolving toward perfection as well—the *glorified* man. Many things we find to be odd or difficult to comprehend, often turn out with time to be brilliant in design.

CAMBRIAN EXPLOSION (BIOLOGICAL BIG BANG)

Assiduous collecting up cliff faces yields zigzags, minor oscillations, and the very occasional slight accumulation of change—over millions of years, at a rate too slow to account for all the prodigious change that has occurred in evolutionary history. When we do see the introduction of evolutionary novelty, it usually shows up with a bang . . .![19]

Niles Eldredge

The scientific principle of *natura non facit saltum* is a principle that Darwin held to fervently. Darwin argued that nature makes no jumps; only God does!

According to strict Darwinian evolution, species evolve from a lower form to a higher form through "numerous, successive, slight modifications."[20] The fossil record, therefore, should be filled with transitional, intermediate forms. Every geological formation, every stratum, should be full of such links. My backyard should be filled with such links!

The case is quite the opposite; there is a troubling lack of transitional or intermediate links. At one time it was thought that Java Man or Lucy or Neanderthal Man were intermediate links, but this is no longer the case. In fact, Neanderthal Man lived alongside Homo Sapien man, modern man.

The fossil record is full of examples of *micro*evolution, but the fossil record lacks irrefutable examples of *macro*evolution. There are different types of gulls, but they are still gulls; there are different types of fruit-flies but they are still fruit-flies; there are different types of woodwablers, but they are still woodwablers; there are different types of honeycreepers, but they are still honeycreepers; there are different types of lizards, but they are still lizards; there are many different types of horses, but they are still horses.

The same applies with human beings. As Richard Milton, a British science journalist, explains:

> *The position today is that all fossil remains which were previously assigned some intermediate status between apes and humans have later been definitely reassigned into the categories of either extinct ape or human, and this reassignment has been accepted by all but the most fanatical devotees of this or that fossil . . . the missing link is still missing.*[21]

Or as explained by Harvard paleontologist Stephen Gould:

> *The extreme rarity of transitional forms in the fossil record persists as the trade secret of paleontology. The evolutionary trees that adorn our textbooks have data only at the tips and nodes of their branches; the rest is inference, however reasonable, not the evidence of fossils.*[22]

So how do we explain macroevolution? The theory of *punctuated equilibrium* comes to the rescue, *comes to fill the gap*.[23] Since there is a troubling lack of transitional or intermediate fossils to explain the evolution of man, Darwinian evolution has been revised by many scientists. They have adopted the theory of *punctuated equilibrium*. The Cambrian explosion is an example of this.

Five hundred and thirty million years ago the fossil record was inhabited by single or simple celled organisms such as algae and bacteria. As we approach the 530 million year time period, multi-cellular organism such as sponges appear, and then an explosion takes place, an explosion that takes place within a *geological instant*, five to ten million years. Not only is there an explosion of cells and development, but there is also an explosion of genetic information within organisms. The geological record radically changes from simple celled (five or less) organisms to organisms with fifty or more cell types. The first *bodied animals* appear: Insects, crustaceans, and chordates are found for the first time, organisms with new structures and new functions.

How do we explain this explosion or jump? It is contrary to traditional evolution! Statisticians and scientists—such as William Dembski have estimated the probability of such an explosion of evolutionary change from algae and bacteria to insects, crustaceans, mollusks, and chordates at being 10 to the 150th—that is, 10 with 150 zeros behind it. That is for all practical purposes a miracle or an impossibility! It is easier to ascribe this explosion and this development of new knowledge and new structures and functions to a God than to random chance. *Nature makes no jumps; only God does!*

What about human life? After the Cambrian explosion we have the emergence of the human species, without any forerunner, with code and symbol processing systems, with goal and intention seeking manifestations. We have the birth of subjective awareness, conceptual thought, and self-awareness.

The appearance of the human person is more attributable to a God-directed evolution than atheistic evolution! *Nature makes no jumps; only God does!*

THE BIRTH OF MOLECULAR BIOLOGY

The new field of molecular biology and the new field of comparative biochemistry have almost closed the book on transitory or intermediary species. By studying the sequential arrangement of proteins, the differences of protein sequences in living species, one can determine the relatedness of species. Studies in molecular biology have shown no evidence of transitory or intermediate species. As Michael Denton explains:

> *Thousand of different sequences, protein and nucleic acid, have now been compared in hundreds of different species but never has any sequence been found to be in any sense the lineal descendant or ancestor of any other sequence. . . . It is now well established that the pattern of diversity at a molecular level conforms to a highly ordered hierarchic system. Each class at a molecular level is unique, isolated and unlinked by intermediaries. . . .* [24]

Molecular biology has almost put to rest the idea that evolution takes place in a slow and random process. *Nature makes no jumps; only God does!*

THE UN-EVOLVED

Molecular biology has now been able to confirm that there are many biological structures that have never experienced evolution. Cilium, for example, occurs in nearly all animal species, protozoans, and plants. Yet its molecular structure has never evolved; its basic structure has always been maintained! As the molecular biologist Michael Denton explains:[25]

> *Every cilium that has been examined to date has been found to possess essentially the same basic structure. . . . There is no hint anywhere of any sort of structure halfway to the complex molecular organization of these fascinating microhairs through which their evolution might have occurred.*

The same applies to the cell and the genetic code. Not only is there, as mentioned earlier, not enough time to explain the evolution of the cell, there is in fact no evidence to support that it ever evolved.

> *As a result of one of the most remarkable discoveries in molecular biology, it is now known [that the genetic code within a cell is] a unique and invariant system of rules which is identical in every cell on earth. No cell has ever been found that departs in any significant way from the universal pattern of the code. . . . Like cilia, and like so many of the characteristics found in living things on earth, the genetic code is not led up to gradually through a sequence of transitional forms.*

Why did these structures not evolve or have precursors? Design over chance is favored. A designer, God, over randomness is favored.

OTHER EXAMPLES

The Cretaceous period marks an explosion in the existence of higher plant life. In less than fifty million years we have an explosion of vegetative life, similar in emergence to the Cambrian explosion—a kind of *Cretaceous explosion.*

Four hundred million years ago we have an explosion of fish groups. Three hundred and fifty million years ago we have an explosion of amphibian life.

The same pattern of jumps or explosions, without the appearance of transitional forms or intermediaries, is found in the case of reptilian and mammalian groups.

Given traditional evolution you would expect to find transitional and intermediary fossils in every location, even in your backyard.

Only jumps can explain evolution, and in the spirit of Darwin, only God makes jumps! Either macroevolution is a failed theory, a fraud, or it is an act of God's work.

ATHEISTIC EVOLUTION, AN ACT OF FAITH

[Darwin's] general theory, that all life on earth had originated and evolved by a gradual successive accumulation of fortuitous mutations, is still, as it was in Darwin's time, a highly speculative hypothesis entirely without direct factual support and very far from that self-evident axiom some of its more aggressive advocates would have us believe.[26]

Michael Denton

Atheistic evolution requires a leap of faith.

Fossil records alone will never suffice to explain evolution since fossil records lack the soft-body components of species, and without the soft-body components, the fossil record will always be conjectural.

Evolution from one species to another has never been (at the macro level) seen as it actually occurs. Studies in common genealogy, comparative embryology, biochemistry and anatomy, have never been able to find intermediaries or even proofs for macroevolution. Homology is a tentative endeavor.[27]

And in terms of the *pre-biotic soup* where life was supposed to have evolved from, there is not a single shred of evidence![28]

Atheistic evolution has its own version of the Old Testament, the writings of Anaximander, Empedocles, Democritus, Epicurus, and Homer. Within these writings we have examples of natural selection and the evolution of life from water to land—from lower forms to higher forms.

In the writings of Aristotle we have the origin of a hierarchy of taxa with its own version of an evolutionary tree—similar to that found in modern science (i.e., Kingdom, Phylum, Class, Order, Family, Genus, Species). In many ways Aristotle is the father of cladism, typology, and taxonomy.

Atheistic evolution has its own heretics, those that deviate slightly from the traditional interpretation of evolution. Scientists such as Klammerer, Steel, Goldschmidt, and Schindewolf are viewed as heretical because they dare to question certain aspects of Darwinism.[29]

Evolution, whether atheistic or God-driven, requires a leap of faith at the *macro* level.

Atheistic evolution, creationism, or theistic evolution are all acts of faith.

NOTES

1. Richard Dawkins denies the need for God to explain evolution in *Climbing Mount Improbable*, 77. This, as seen, and will be seen, leaves Dawkins in a precarious position, for if evolution is more likely the product of intelligent design, atheism collapses.

2. William Dembski, *Intelligent Design* (Dover Grove: Inter Varsity, 1999) 106f.

3. For a more detailed analysis of intelligent design the following is recommended, with one provision—as a Catholic I do not see, nor does my Church, any conflict between evolution and intelligent design. In fact, evolution, as I argue, is a powerful proof for intelligent design. Furthermore, intelligent design is not a science, but a proof for the existence of God in the Catholic sense: "convincing and converging" arguments favoring the existence of God over his non-existence. William Dembski, Sean McDowell, *Understanding Intelligent Design* (Eugene: Harvest House, 2008); Michael Behe, William Dembski, Stephen Meyer, *Science and Evidence for Design in the Universe* (San Francisco: Ignatius, 2000); Michael Behe, *The Edge of Evolution* (New York: Free Press, 2006); Denyse O'Leary, *By Design or by Chance* (Minneapolis: Augsburg, 2004); William Dembski & Jonathan Wells, *The Design of Life* (Dallas: Foundations for Thought and Ethics, 2007); William Dembski, *The Design Inference* (Cambridge: Cambridge University Press, 1998); Antony Flew, *How the World's Most Notorious Atheist Changed His Mind* (New York: HarperOne, 2007); Thomas Woodard, *Darwin Strikes Back* (Grand Rapids: Baker Books, 2006); Jonathan Wells, *The Politically Incorrect Guide to Darwinism and Intelligent Design* (Washington: Regnery, 2006); Richard Halvorson, "Questioning the Orthodoxy: Intelligent Design Theory Is Breaking the Scientific Monopoly of Darwinism," *Harvard Political Review* (May 14): 2002. Daniel Dennett's *Darwin's Dangerous Idea* and Dawkins' *The God Delusion* and his *The Blind Watchmaker* oppose intelligent design, but primarily from the point of view of evolution.

4. Antony Flew, "My Pilgrimage from Atheism to Theism," *Philosophia Christi*, vol. 6, no. 2, 2004, 201.

5. Ibid., *There is A God*), 88. "Biology is the study of complicated things that give the appearance of having been designed for a purpose." The atheist biologist Francis Crick, the co-discoverer of the DNA double Helix, likewise had to admit: "Biologists must constantly keep in mind that what they see was not designed, but rather, evolved."

6. Cited in Roy Abraham Varghese, "The Supreme Science," *Viewpoints* (December 16, 2004): 35A.

7. Michael Denton, *Evolution: A Theory in Crisis* (Chevy Chase: Adler and Adler), 1986, 264.

8. Richard Dawkins, *The Blind Watchmaker* (New York: Norton, 1986), 1.

9. Francis Crick, *What Mad Pursuit* (New York: Basic Books, 1988), 138.

10. Daniel Dennett in *Breaking the Spell* (New York: Penguin Books, 2007), 62, admits to the extraordinary efficiency of the human body.

11. For a study of the cell and its relation to intelligent design I recommend the following: Fazale Rana, *The Cell's Design* (Grand Rapids: Baker Books, 2008). Again, one provision must be made. Catholicism in no way views intelligent design and evolution as opposing theories. Even Richard Dawkins calculates the origins of DNA at a billion to one, *The God Delusion*, 138.

12. Cf. Richard Dawkins, *The God Delusion*, 145.

13. It is this argument that Richard Dawkins has to back into reluctantly in *The God Delusion*, 137-138. When push comes to shove Dawkins has to admit the pos-

sibility for the existence of God, no matter how offensive it is to him, *The God Delusion*, 51. The words of Dawkins are exactly: "However improbable the origin of life might be, we know it happened because we are here," *The God Delusion*, 137.

14. Richard Swinburne, "Design Defended," *Think* (Spring 2004), 17.

15. Antony Flew, *There is a God*, 121.

16. Following quotes come from William Paley, *Natural Theology* (New York: Oxford University Press, 2006), 8, 12, 9.

17. Micheal Behe, *Darwin's Black Box* (New York: Free Press, 2006), 39.

18. Denton, 157–195; 174.

19. Niles Eldredge, *Reinventing Darwin* (New York: Wiley, 1995), 95.

20. Charles Darwin, *On the Origin of Species* (Cambridge: Harvard University Press, 1964), 189.

21. Richard Milton, *Shattering the Myths of Darwinism* (Rochester: Park Street Press, 1997), 199–208.

22. Stephen Gould, "Evolution's Erratic Pace," *Natural History*, vol. 86, no. 5 (May 1977): 12–16.

23. Stephen Gould, "Punctuated Equilibria: An Alternative to Phyletic Gradualism" in *Models of Paleobiology*, ed. T.J.M. Schopf (San Francisco: Freeman, Cooper and Co., 1973), 82–115.

24. Denton, 289–290.

25. Denton, 108–109; P. Satir, "How Cilia Move," *Scientific American* (1974): 231 (4), 44-52; A. Frey-Wyssling, *Comparitive Organellography of the Cytoplasm* (New York: Springer-Verlag, 1973), 65f.

26. Denton, 77.

27. Denton, 141–155.

28. Denton, 261.

29. Cf. A. Koestler, *The Midwife Toad* (London: Hutchinson Publishing Co., 1971); R. Goldschmidt, *The Material Basis for Evolution* (New Haven: Yale University Press, 1940); O. H. Schindewolf., cited in B. Rensch, Evolution above the Species (New York: Columbia University Press, 1959).

Intelligent Design— A Cosmological Look

The more I examine the universe and study the details of its architecture, the more evidence I find that the universe in some sense knew we were coming.[1]

Freeman Dyson

THE BIG BANG THEORY

The *big bang theory* argues that the beginning of the universe had its origins in an extremely compact, dense, hot mass, a mass of primordial matter made up of protons, neutrons, and electrons in a sea of radiation. The expanding and cooling universe developed into gravitational, electromagnetic, strong and weak nuclear forces, and what would eventually become our modern conception of the universe.

The theory of the *oscillating universe* is a variation on the traditional *big bang* theory. This theory argues that after the *big bang* the universe expanded and will continue to expand to a point where it can no longer expand (due to the universe's density or concentration of mass); once this point of expansion has reached its capacity, the universe's expansion will eventually stop and the universe will begin contracting until it collapses back into its original primordial state, preparing to explode and expand again. Thus the universe, according to this theory, is seen as continually expanding and contracting, continually oscillating, with no real beginning or end.

The great dilemma with the *big bang theory* is that it cannot explain what happened *before* the big bang. In other words, where did this compact, dense primordial matter come from and what caused it to explode? One is left with the reality that either the universe always existed, oscillating, or God created it. One is left with either an uncreated primordial state of matter (*ylem*) or a God who is the source of this primordial state of matter.

It is interesting to note that some scientists have argued that if one were to rewind the expansion of the universe backwards to its origin, one would come to *a singularity, a point* which has to be considered an origin but which is outside space, time, and the domain of the laws of nature. *God is beyond space and time and is not bound to the laws of nature!*

While there are several versions of the *Big Bang world*, the end results are the same. God's existence is favored over his non-existence, for all things that are in being in our world and according to our personal experiences are so because someone or something made it so!

Either the world always existed or the world had a source for its being. Richard Dawkins sarcastically snarls, "Who created God?" If Y were God and X created Y, then Y would no longer be God, X would! And if X were created by W, then X would no longer be God, W would. This is what we call an infinite regress. The problem with an infinite regress is twofold: 1) It is contrary to our experience of reality, for all things that exist in our sphere of comprehension exist because someone or something put it into existence; 2) An infinite regress can only be stopped by that which is *existence itself, subsistent existence*, God. (Richard Dawkins fails to comprehend infinite regress.)

FINELY TUNED UNIVERSE

We live on a privileged planet. We live in a finely tuned universe. In fact, the universe is so finely tuned that any slight variation in its structure would make life impossible.

Things that are finely tuned are more a product of design than chance or coincidence. That which is tuned is so because it was tuned by a tuner. What or who is this tuner, if not God?

Let us look at some of these finely tuned features that make life possible.

- If the age of the universe were older than it is, no stable burning star-types, in the right part of the galaxy, would be around. If the universe were younger, there would be no stars. In both cases, there would be no life.
- Protons are 1836 times larger than electrons. If they were a little bigger or smaller, human life would not be possible. If the ratio of electron to proton mass were larger or smaller, chemical bonding would be insufficient for the chemistry of life. If the number of protons to the number of electrons were

larger or smaller, electromagnetism would dominate gravity, preventing galaxy, star, and planet formation.

- If the ratio of neutron mass to proton mass were higher, the formation of life would be impossible. If the ratio were lower, the universe would be an amalgamation of black holes.
- If the mass of the *neutrino* were larger, galaxy clusters and galaxies would be too dense to exist. If smaller, galaxies would never have formed.
- Protons, with their positive electrical charge, balance out electrons, with their negative electrical charge. If this was not so, life would not be possible.
- If the decay rate of protons were greater, life would not be able to survive the accompanying release of radiation. If smaller, the universe would not have enough matter for life.
- If the *strong nuclear force constant* were larger, there would be no hydrogen for life to form. If smaller, no elements heavier than hydrogen would form, and thus the formation of life would not be possible. If the *weak nuclear force* constant were larger, stars would convert too much matter into heavy elements, making life impossible. If smaller, stars would convert too little matter into heavy elements making life unattainable.
- If the expansion rate of the universe were larger there would be no galaxies. If smaller, the universe would have collapsed.
- If the ratio of *exotic matter mass* to *ordinary matter mass* were larger, the universe would collapse. If smaller, there would be no existent galaxies.
- If water did not exist on this planet in three states—ice, water, and gas—life could not exist.
- If the polarity of the water molecule were smaller or greater, life could not develop.
- If *white dwarf binaries* were too few in number, there would be an insufficient amount of fluorine for life. If too many, planetary orbits would be too unstable for life.
- If the size of the *relativistic dilation factor* were larger or smaller, certain chemical reactions necessary for life would not be operational.
- If there were not the right combination of gases in the universe (even a slight variation) life would not be sustainable. Either an extreme greenhouse effect or an atmosphere bombarded by cosmic radiation would result.
- If the rate of *carbon to oxygen nuclear energy level ratio* were larger, the universe would have an insufficient amount of oxygen for life. If smaller, the universe would have an insufficient amount of carbon for life.
- If supernovae eruptions were too close, or too frequent, or too late, radiation would exterminate life on earth. If too distant, too infrequent, or too soon, then the necessary heavy elements to produce planets would be missing.

- If the *initial uniformity of radiation* were more uniform, there would be no life. If less uniform, the universe would be made up of *black holes* and empty space. There would be no life.
- If the earth's magnetic field were weaker, our planet would be devastated by radiation. If the magnetic field were stronger, we would be devastated by electromagnetic storms.
- If the ratio of the *electromagnetic force to the gravitational force constant* were larger, the sun would be among the smallest stars, making stellar burning insufficient to support life. If smaller, the sun would be larger than most stars, making the production of heavy elements inadequate for life.
- If the gravitational force in the universe were larger, stars would be too unstable for life. If smaller, the stars would be too cool for nuclear fusion, and therefore insufficient for the existence of life.
- A slight change in the orbits of the planets would impact our moon, and therefore impact our earth's gravity to such an extent, that life would not be sustainable. If the moon were a different size, wild fluctuations in temperature would follow, tides would be impacted, the proper mixing of nutrients in the oceans would be inadequate, and life would be unsustainable.
- If the average distance between galaxies were larger, there would be an insufficient amount of matter to form stars. If smaller, the sun's orbit would be unstable, making life impossible.
- If we were much further from the sun in our solar system, the oceans would be ice, and life would not exist. If we were much closer, the oceans would be boiling or vaporizing.
- If the average distance between stars were larger, rocky planets could not form. If smaller, planetary orbits would be too unstable to sustain life.
- If the density of galaxy clusters were denser, the sun's orbit would be disrupted. If less dense, there would be a lack of necessary material for the formation of stars. Life would not be achievable.
- If the sun's rays were more red or more blue (as seen in the flames that come off of logs in a fireplace) photosynthesis, the mechanism that allows for plants to exist, would cease and we would cease to exist as well. A smaller or larger sun would make the planet inhabitable.
- If the velocity of light were faster, stars would be too luminous to support life. If slower, stars would be insufficiently luminous to sustain life.
- We live in the right kind of galaxy. Elliptical galaxies do not have the necessary heavy elements necessary for life, and irregular galaxies are prone to supernova explosions. Our spiral galaxy is ideal for fostering life. Jupiter's size and gaseous nature protects the earth from comets; and Mars, being at the edge of the asteroid belt, protects the earth from incoming asteroids.[2]

Intelligent design makes possible the scientific method, makes possible physics, mathematics, and all the sciences. Without an implied order, or implied laws of nature, there would be nothing other than chaos! Evolution and the mystery of the universe is far more a product of a divine orderer, an intelligent designer, than simply chance. A finely tuned universe is much more likely the work of an intelligent designer than anything else!

> *Everyone who is seriously engaged in the pursuit of science becomes convinced that the laws of nature manifest the existence of a spirit vastly superior to that of men, and one in the face of which we with our modest powers must feel humble. . . . Whoever has undergone the intense experience of successful advances in the domain of science is moved by profound reverence for the rationality made manifest in existence . . . the grandeur of reason incarnate in existence. . . . The deeply emotional conviction of the presence of a superior reasoning power, which is revealed in the incomprehensible universe, forms my idea of God.[3]*
>
> *Albert Einstein*

NOTES

1. Freeman Dyson, *Disturbing the Universe* (New York: Harper and Row, 1979), 250, cited in Flew, *There is a God*.

2. Cf. Hugh Ross, *The Creator and the Cosmos* (Colorodo Springs: NavPress, 2001).

3. Cf. *Albert Einstein, Ideas and Opinions*, trans. Sonja Bargmann (New York: Dell, 1973), 49; *Jammer, Einstein and Religion*, 93. Einstein, *The Quotable Einstein*, ed., Alice Calaprice (Princeton: Princeton University Press, 2005), 196–196.

VII

Origin of Life Question

More than 30 years of experimentation on the origin of life in the field of chemical and molecular evolution have led to a better perception of the immensity of the problem of the origin of life on earth rather than to its solution. At present all discussions on principle theories and experiments in the field [end up] in a confession of ignorance.[1]

Klaus Dose

An honest man, armed with all the knowledge available to us now, could only state that in some sense, the origin of life appears at the moment to be almost a miracle, so many are the conditions which would have had to have been satisfied to get it going.[2]

Francis Crick, co-discoverer of the DNA Double Helix

The origin of life question has never been answered by science.

Non-living materials cannot produce living materials. A universe of mindless, non-living materials cannot produce living beings with intrinsic ends, self-replicating capabilities, and a coded chemistry.[3] Life is brought about by life, by preexisting life structures.[4]

Is God or chance the answer to the origin of life question? I favor God.

NOTES

1. Klaus Dose, "The Origin of Life: More Questions than Answers," *Interdisciplinary Science Reviews* (1988): 13, 348.

2. Francis Crick, *Life Itself* (New York: Simon and Schuster, 1981), 88.

3. Antony Flew, *There is a God*, 124.

4. Protobiologists have produced theories (i.e., abiogenesis) to explain the evolution of non-living matter to living matter. Yet this is simply a theory and has never been validated through experimentation.

VIII

Consciousness

Many attempts have been made to explain consciousness. Some scientists and neurologists have speculated about consciousness in terms of patterns of electromagnetic activation, brain wave sequences, brain wave collapses, synaptic tunnels, synaptic passages, neural networks, neural excitations, neurotransmitters, quantum waves, quantum discontinuities, and quantum cytoskeletal states. Others have promoted the belief that consciousness comes from the interaction of bosons and fermions, biological oscillators, and bio-plasma charged particles. Still others have tried to explain consciousness by the trajectory of particles, "subtle energies," the excitation of condensates, and the working in unison of molecules. All forms of electro-chemical processes have been postulated.[1]

I am conscious. I am matter. How can matter, which has no consciousness, be put together to produce consciousness?

To make the point more concrete, Roy Varghese gives the following example:

Think for a minute of a marble table in front of you. Do you think that, given a trillion years or infinite time, this table could suddenly or gradually become conscious, aware of its surroundings, aware of its identity the way you are? It is simply inconceivable that this would or could happen. And the same goes for any kind of matter. Once you understand the nature of matter, of mass-energy, you realize that, by its very nature, it could never become 'aware,' never 'think,' never say 'I.' But the atheist position is that, at some point in the history of the universe, the impossible and the inconceivable took place. Undifferentiated matter (here we include energy), at some point, became 'alive,' then conscious, then conceptually proficient, then an 'I.' But returning to our table, we see why

36

this is simply laughable. The table has none of the properties of being conscious and, given infinite time, it cannot 'acquire' such properties.[2]

Random, chance evolution cannot explain the complexity of consciousness. If the cell could not have evolved in 3.7 billion years, consciousness certainly could not have evolved in 3.7 billion years. The evolution of consciousness would require an astronomical jump. But as we know, from our friend Darwin: Nature makes no jumps; only God does!

The complexity of consciousness favors a God-driven evolution rather than a random, blind evolution. The source of consciousness favors God.

Where does the psyche [consciousness] come from? The phenomenon of consciousness proves that, at a certain time, our psyche certainly begins to exist in us. The laws of physics prove that the psyche [consciousness] cannot be the product of physical, chemical or biological processes. Therefore, the origin of our psyche is transcendent to the physical reality. We can then identify with God the necessary Cause of the existence of the psyche, being such Cause transcendent.[3]

Marco Biagini

NOTES

1. Cf. www.scaruffi.com/tat/consc3. The following are examples of speculative theories that have attempted to explain the unexplainable. David Chalmers, *The Conscious Mind* (Oxford University Press, 1996); John Eccles, *The Evolution of the Brain* (Routledge, 1989). Nick Herbert, *The Elemental Mind* (Dutton, 1993); Michael Lockwood, *Mind, Brain and the Quantum* (Basil Blackwell, 1989); Alfred Whitehead, *Modes of Thought* (Macmillan, 1939); Fred Wolf, *Mind into Matter* (Moment Point, 2001).

2. Roy Varghese, *There is a God*, appendix I, 163.

3. Marco Biagini, "Mind and Brain," *Center of Scientific Divulgation about Consciousness*, cf. xoomer.virgilio.it/fedeescienza/mindandbrain, 19–20.

IX

Christ-point Explosion

I have never found a better expression than 'religious' for this trust in the rational nature of reality and of its peculiar accessibility to the human mind. Where this trust is lacking science degenerates into an uninspired procedure. Let the devil care if the priests make capital out of this. There is no remedy for that.[1]

Einstein

Just as the Cambrian explosion forever changed the world, the incarnation of Christ[2] brought about a new outpouring of grace-oriented potential that forever changed the world. When we look at the technological and scientific advancements that have taken place since the Incarnation of Christ (within the short period of 2000 years), one is dumbfounded in trying to explain the explosion that has taken place in technical and scientific advancements. Exponential growth factors and the natural processes of evolution, cultural or otherwise, are insufficient to explain the advancements we take for granted today. Only an intelligent designer, only the power of a *God-force*, grace, can explain these advancements.

The grace-formed insights and Catholic mindset, predisposed to the laws of nature, to a divine orderer, provided for an explosion in the advancement of the sciences and humanities never before seen.

JESUITS

When we look at just one religious order within the Catholic Church, the Jesuit order, we cannot but be overwhelmed by the Catholic hunger for scientific knowledge that was initiated by the Incarnation of Christ. When examining the history of science between 900 BC (before the birth of Christ) and 1800 AD (after the birth of Christ), we are amazed to find that five percent of history's greatest mathematicians are recognized as Jesuit priests—this is particularly impressive when you consider that the Jesuit order did not exist until the fifteenth century.

Thirty-five craters on the moon are named after Jesuit scientists.[3]

MONKS

The monks and their monasteries were responsible for fostering a common language (Latin), for protecting, copying, and preserving ancient texts, for developing and elevating astronomy, music, arithmetic, geometry, logic, grammar, and rhetoric to heights never before achieved. They developed a common script with letters, punctuation, spaces, and paragraphs. Through Cathedral Schools they preserved and reproduced for all generations the works of Aristotle, Cicero, Seneca, Lucan, Pliny, Statius, Trogas, Pompeius, Virgil, Horace, Martial, Suetonius, Plato, Ovid, etc. Upon the request of Pope Damasus I, they compiled a book which would eventually be known as the Bible.[4]

With over 37,000 monasteries, the monks, known as the *agriculturists of Europe*, saved and perfected the art of agriculture and laid the foundation for industry. They transformed much of Europe, such as modern day Germany, from a forest into a country, while at the same time planting and conserving trees in what we would now call *preserves*. The monks were the first environmentalists.[5]

The monks introduced crops, developed new production methods (such as complicated irrigation systems), raised better producing bees, produced better fruits and vegetables, invented champagne, perfected the brewing of beer and the making of cheese. They reared cattle and horses, developed the corn trade, managed and perfected wine through the vineyards, and even developed salmon fisheries.[6]

The monks became the great technical advisors to the West, and became rightly so the fathers of what would eventually become the Industrial Revolution. They were the leading iron producers, and the leading miners of salt, lead, iron, and marble. They were masters of glasswork and master clock workers. They were among the first to use the byproducts of their iron production as fertilizer for crops. [7]

The monks would become the educators of Europe by opening schools for all who desired an education, no matter what their economic or social status was. The world's first comprehensive school system for the populace was created by the monks, by the Catholic Church. Individual monasteries became known for their specialties. St. Benignus of Dijon was known for its education in medicine, the monks of St. Gall were known for their painting and engraving. The German monasteries were known for their work in teaching Greek, Hebrew and Arabic. Others schools were known for astronomy, philosophy, law, rhetoric, mathematics, geometry, metallurgy, agriculture, navigation, food production, landscaping and preservation.[8]

THE CHURCH IN GENERAL

The Catholic Church invented the university system for those who desired an education, whether wealthy or poor, whether high class or low class. All were offered an education, if they so desired one. Schools dedicated to preserving and cultivating knowledge were opened throughout Europe by the Church, some of the most famous being Oxford, Cambridge, Paris, Salamanca, and Bologna. The university system was made up of professors that taught classes from prepared texts, used the Socratic or dialectical method, and ultimately conferred degrees—Bachelor of Arts and Master's degrees.

Under the protection of the popes, the greatest promoters of education the world has ever seen, universities taught civil and canon law, art, philosophy, theology, ethics, geometry, logic, and many other subjects.

No institution or group has done more for the education of peoples than the popes and the Catholic Church. No institution that has ever existed has done more for the advancement, preservation, and cultivation of knowledge than the Catholic Church.[9]

The very nature of the Catholic Church made it most suitable for education, particularly in the sciences. The Catholic embrace of the natural order made science perfectly apt for Catholic minds. The very hunger for finding God in his creation, for finding the handprint of God in creation, propelled Catholics to become scientists.

Despite the sad Galileo incident, the Catholic Church has done more than any organization in the history of the world for the advancement of science. Roger Bacon, a Franciscan, and Bishop Grosseteste are often referred to as the forerunners of the modern scientific method. The priest Giambattista Riccioli laid the foundation and principles that would be responsible for all of modern astronomy. The priest Roger Boscovich is often referred to as the father and forerunner of atomic physics, the father of modern atomism.[10] The priest Athanasius Kircher was a master chemist who debunked alchemy and astrology and laid the foundation of Egyptology. Kircher made the interpreting of the Rosetta stone possible.[11] The priest Nicolas Zucchi invented the reflecting telescope.[12] Jean Buridan, the Catholic professor at the Sorbonne, laid the foundation for much of Newton's work, particularly his first law. The priest Nicolaus Steno is acknowledged as a pioneer in modern geology and is considered the father of stratigraphy.

The monk Gregor Mendel became the father of genetics and the laws of inheritance. The priest Francisco Lana-Terzi is known as the father of flight. The Abbot Richard of Wallingford is known as among the greatest pioneers of Western trigonometry.

Antoine Laurent Lavoisier is associated with the *revolution in chemistry*, Erwin Schrodinger with wave mechanics, Blaise Pascal for his theory of probability and the mechanical adding machine, Enrico Fermi with atomic physics, Marcello Malpighi with microscopic anatomy, and Alexander Fleming with penicillin. The list is exhaustive!

The Catholic Church is rightly acknowledged as the *father of modern science*.[13]

The Catholic Church would be responsible for the spread of knowledge by the creation and distribution of massive encyclopedias of knowledge.[14] The Church would spread this scientific knowledge worldwide through its missionaries—no other institution has done more to spread knowledge and science worldwide![15]

The Church's genius in the arts and its preservation is unequalled. From its Cathedrals, its stain-glassed windows, to its painted ceilings and portraitures, the Catholic Church's artistic heritage is beyond comparison. From its obsession with proportion and beauty in architecture, art, and music, to its obsession with the divine order, the Church brought the world beauty never before imagined. From Giotto, Masaccio, Donatello, Brunelleschi, Titian, Tintoretto, Bellini, Botticelli, Caravaggio, Ghiberti, Bondone, Cimabue, Bramante, Michelangelo, to Raphael, the artistic intellect has never been equaled. All this was done under the patronage of the popes, such as Pope Julius II and Leo X.[16] Literary giants and music giants such as Shakespeare, Dante, Beethoven, Mozart, Verdi are so numerous that there would not be enough space within this book to discuss them all.

The world's greatest explorers were Catholic. Almagro, Alvarado, Avila, Balboa, Bartolomeu, Benalcazar, Buttuta, Cabot, Cano, Cartier, Chaplain, Columbus, Cortez, Federmann, Grijalva, Irala, Legazpi, Magellan, Mendana de Neira, Mendoza, Ojeda, Pigafetta, Pinzon, Pizarrro, Polo, Ponce de Leon, Quesada, Quros, Torres, Vasco de Gama, Velasquez de Cuellar, etc., explored, discovered, and mapped the world.[17]

Western civilization owes its sense of international law and civil law to the Church's legacy. The priest Francisco de Vitoria is often referred to as the father of modern international law.[18] In his work on the mistreatment of natives by the Spanish in the *new world* Francisco affirmed the belief that there are innate natural laws that make all people equally free—whether baptized or not—equally having the right to life and liberty. One has a right to one's own unique culture, and the right to property. Vitoria would be responsible for laying down what we now call the *law of nations*, laws among nations in peacetime and war.

The foundations of modern civil law are often attributed to the monk Gratian in his *Concordance of Discordant Canons* (ca. 1140). Scholars see in canon law the first systematic collection of law and its philosophical implications.[19] The pagan principles of *blood duels*, *trial by battle*, and *trial by fire and water*, were abolished.

Taking the best of the ancient world, and reformulating it within the concept of the person as the image of God, the Church would elevate law to unheard of standards. Natural rights and universal moral laws and claims based on the natural order would become the norm for all nations under Catholic tutelage. A violation of the law was seen as a violation of the natural moral order, a violation to the intended harmony assumed between persons, and persons and creation.

The Church affirmed the right to property, self-defense, and equal protection under the law. Trails were to be rational, systematic procedures that not only meted out justice, but also took into account mitigating circumstances (such as insanity, duress)—a revolution for its time.[20]

Way before Adam Smith, the foundations for modern economic systems or what has become known as *scientific economics* were laid down by the Catholic Church. Abbot Etienne Bonnot de Condillac, the abbot Robert Jacques Turgot, and Francois Quesnay are often referred to as the *founders of the economic sciences*. Nicolas Oresme is considered the founding father of monetary economics; he would lay the foundation for what would evolve into Gershan's law. Cardinal Cajetan would become known as the founder of the *expectation theory* in economics. Pierre de Jean Olivi, a Franciscan clergyman, would become known as the founder of the *value theory of economics*. The abbot Ferdinando Galiani would be instrumental in laying the foundations for the idea that utility and scarcity are determinants to price.[21]

The Catholic Church revolutionized the world by bringing to it a charitable spirit. The Catholic Church is the world's largest systematic, gratuitous, empathetic, merciful, charitable organization that has ever existed. Basing itself on the sacredness of human life, the uniqueness of the individual, and a preferential option for the poor, the elderly, the widowed, and the ill, the Church would revolutionize the world. They would abolish the pagan and barbarian practices of infanticide, abortion, euthanasia, and gladiatorial games.

The early Church was known for providing shelter for travelers and the homeless, for providing clothing and food for the poor, and for establishing hospices for the dying. The Church provided for the first systematic, gratuitous, institutionalized care of widows and orphans. During times of plagues, Catholics were renowned for staying and risking their lives burying the dead and caring for the ill.

The Catholic Church invented the hospital! The modern system where institutions of care are staffed by doctors and nurses is a gift of Catholicism to the world. Doctors diagnosed illnesses and prescribed remedies. By the fourth century every major city in Europe had a hospital.[22]

The Church would elevate the status of women to levels unheard of. No institution in the records of history has done more for women than the Catholic Church. It is the Church that gave women equal protection and status in marriage — holding men equally responsible and punishable for adultery and fornication. Women became the founders and abbesses of self-governing religious orders and communities. Women religious built and ran their own schools, convents, colleges, hospitals, hospices, and orphanages. The world's largest religious television network, EWTN, was founded, constructed, and led by a simple nun, Mother Angelica.

The Church has produced more famous women than any other institution. The list of canonized women saints alone is a mark of this truth.

The Church is made up of humans, not walking gods. The Church has a long legacy of sin. But the fact remains: *No institution in world history has done more for the advancement of human beings than the Catholic Church!*

Christianity's or more particularly Catholicism's worldview was and is perfectly suited for science and the development of humankind!

The Catholic Church is rightly acknowledged as the *father of modern science and the father of the best in the modern world.*[23]

NOTES

1. Albert Einstein, *Lettres a Maurice Solovine reproduits en facsimile et traduits en francais* (Paris: Gauthier-Vilars, 1956), 102–103.

2. Chapter IX illustrates this Christ-point Explosion.

3. I am deeply indebted to the work done by Thomas E. Woods, *How the Catholic Church Built Western Civilization* (Washington: Regnery, 2005), 101.

4. Joseph Lynch, *The Medieval Church* (London: Longman, 1992), 95; Kenneth Clark, *Civilization: A Personal View* (New York: HarperPerennial, 1969), 18; David Knowles, *The Evolution of Medieval Thought*, 2nd ed. (London: Longman, 1988), 69.

5. Henry Goodell, "The Influence of the Monks in Agriculture," in *Goodell Papers*, University of Massachusetts.

6. Woods, 31.

7. Jean Gimpel, *The Medieval Machine: The Industrial Revolution of the Middle Ages* (New York: Holt, Rinehart, and Winston, 1976), 67–68; Reginald Gregoire, *The Monastic Realm* (New York: Rizzoli, 1985), 271.

8. John Henry Cardinal Newman, *Essays and Sketches*, vol. 3, ed. Charles Harrold (New York: Longmans, Green and Co., 1948), 319.

9. Lowrie Daly, *The Medieval University* (New York: Sheed and Ward, 1961), 202.

10. Woods, 106–108.

11. MacDonnell, 12; Erik Iverson, *The Myth of Egypt and its Hieroglyphs* (Copenhagen, 1961), 97–98.

12. Heilbron, 112.

13. Cf. www.adherents.com/people/100_scientists.html.

14. William Ashworth, "Catholicism and Early Modern Science," in Lindberg and Numbers, eds., *God and Nature*, 146.

15. Agustin Udias, *Searching the Heavens and the Earth: The History of Jesuit Observatories* (Dordrecht: Kluwer Academic Publishers, 2003), 53.

16. John Baldwin, *The Scholastic Culture of the Middle Ages* (Lexington: D.C. Heath, 1971), 107.

17. Cf. Daniel Baker, *Explorers and Discoverers of the World* (Washington: Gale Research, 1993); Richard Bohlander, *World Explorers and Discoverers* (New York: Macmillan, 1992); Max Cary, *The Ancient Explorers* (London: Methuen and Company, 1929); Neil Grant, *The Discoverers* (New York: Arco Publishing, 1979); Peter Ryan, *Explorers and Mapmakers* (London: Belitha Press, 1939); Dinah Starkey, *Scholastic Atlas of Exploration* (New York: Harper Collins, 1993).

18. Marcelo Sanchez-Sorondo, Vitoria, *The Original Philosopher of Rights in Hispanic Philosophy in the Age of Discovery*, Kevin White ed. (Washington: Catholic University of America Press, 1997), 66; Lewis Hanke, *All Mankind is One* (DeKalb: Northern Illinois University Press, 1974), 142; James Scott, *The Spanish Origin of International Law* (Washington: Georgetown University Press, 1928), 65.

19. Harold Berman, *Law and Revolution* (Cambridge: Harvard University Press, 1983), 166.

20. Berman, 228; Ibid., 189; Berman, "The Influence of Christianity Upon the Development of Law," *Oklahoma Law Review* 12 (1959): 93, 228; Brian Tierney, *The Idea of Natural Rights* (Grand Rapids: William Eerdmans, 2001); Kenneth Pennington, "The History of Rights in Western Thought," *Emory Law Journal* 47 (1998): 327–52.

21. Cf. Woods, 154–167; Jospeh Schumpeter, *History of Economic Analysis* (New York: Oxford University Press, 1954), 97; Murray Rothland, *An Austrian Perspective on the History of Economic Thought* (Hants: Edward Elgar, 1995), 73–74. The reality that the Catholic spirit brought about the birth of modern science makes a mockery of the words of Michel Onfray, "Monotheism does not really like the rational work of scientists," cf. *In Defense of Atheism*, 67, 81. And to Christopher Hitchens who wrote, "Thanks to the telescope and the microscope, [religion] no longer offers an

explanation of anything important," 282. Dear Christopher, Catholics invented your telescope and perfected your microscope!

22. Alvin Schmidt, *Under the Influence: How Christianity Transformed Civilization* (Grand Rapids: Zondervan, 2001); Michael Davis, *For Altar and Throne* (St. Paul: Remnant, 1997), 13; Gerhard Ulhorn, *Christian Charity in the Ancient Church* (New York: Charles Scribner's Sons, 1883), 264; Cajetan Baluffi, *The Charity and the Church*, trans. Denis Gargan (Dublin: Gill and Son, 1885); William Lecky, *History of European Morals*, vol. 1 (New York: Appleton and Co., 1870); Woods, 170–185, 203–215.

23. Cf. www.adherents.com/people/100_scientists.html.

X

The Mystery of Miracles

Miracles, which occur in all religions, can always be explained in rational terms. Despite this, they leave every explanation subject to questions. These questions leave a person to reflect on that which can often not clearly be explained.

In the Catholic tradition a saint is ordinarily canonized after two miracles. A person, for example, may be suffering from an incurable and irremovable tumor. The x-rays and all the scientific evidence may point to imminent death. The person calls upon the intercession of a particular holy person who has died, with the hope of a cure. Suddenly, what once was there is no longer there: the tumor which once appeared on the x-ray has disappeared.

One of the most famous places to find documented miracles is found in Lourdes, France where it is believed that Mary appeared to a young girl Bernadette. Miracles followed.

Lourdes has a medical bureau with doctors of various religious persuasions, including atheist doctors. If a cure seems to have no medical reason behind it, the case is sent to the International Medical Committee of Lourdes—a committee of specialists. After examination, a pronouncement is made. The doctors never pronounce "a miracle," rather they make the pronouncement that the "cure" is "unexplainable" according to modern science and the modern scientific literature. Since 1905, with the establishment of the medical bureau, sixty-four unexplained phenomena have occurred.[1]

Louis Bouriette was cured of blindness in his left eye on July 28, 1858. Blaisette Cazenave was healed on January 18, 1862 of a chronic infection of the conjunctivae and eyelids. Henri Busque was cured in April 28, 1858 of tuberculosis, purulent adenitis, a septic ulcer, and inflamed lymph glands. Justin Bouhort, unable to walk and suffering from *consumption*, was restored to complete health on July of 1858. Madelaine Rizan was cured on October 17, 1858 of a left-sided paralysis that kept her bedridden. Marie Moreau was restored to health on November 9, 1858 after suffering from blindness. Pierre de Rudder, on July 24, 1908, regained his ability to walk. Joachime Dehant was cured on October 13, 1878 of a gangrenous ulcer on her right leg and a club foot. Elisa Seisson was made well on July 12, 1912, being healed of "chronic bronchitis with severe organic heart disease." Marie Mabille was cured of a "longstanding chronic infection in the right iliac fossa, with vesical and colonic fistulae" on August 8, 1908. Aline Bruyere received her miracle on September 1, 1889, being cured of pulmonary tuberculosis. Anne Jourdain was healed of "tuberculosis with gross apical lesions" on October 10, 1908. Ameilie Chagnon was restored to health on August 21, 1891 after suffering from a long series of "bone diseases," including tuberculous arthritis. Clementine Trouve was healed of tuberculous osteoperiostitis of the right calcaneum on August 21, 1891. Marie Lebranchu and Marie Lemarchand were healed on successive days, the 20th and 21st of August, 1892—Lebranchu being healed of a severe case of pulmonary tuberculosis. Elisa Lesage was cured of ankylosis of the joint in the right knee on August 21, 1892. Sister Marie of the Presentation was saved from starvation on August 15, 1908 after being cured of a case of "chronic gastro-enteritis." Father Cirette was restored to health on August 31, 1893, being cured of a nervous disorder brought about by influenza. Aurelie Huprelle was healed of "cavitating pulmonary tuberculosis" on August 21, 1895. Esther Brachman regained her health on August 21, 1896 after suffering from tuberculosis. Jeanne Tulasne was healed of Pott's Disease on September 8, 1897. Clementine Malot came to Lourdes with a case of "tuberculosis with spitting blood" and was cured on August 8, 1898. Rose Francois was restored to health on August 8, 1899 after a year of suffering from the effects of a "chronic infection of the right arm, with numerous fistulae and gross lymphoedema of the upper arm and forearm." The capuchin priest, Father Salvator was healed of tuberculous peritonitis on June 25, 1900. Sister Macimilien was restored to health after being cured of a hydatid cyst of the liver with phlebitis of the left leg on February 5, 1908. Marie Savoye was healed of rheumatic fever and heart disease (with signs of a mitral lesion) on September 20, 1901. Johanna Bezenac suffered from progressive cachexia, localized lesions, and a severe pneumonia when she was cured on July 2, 1908. Sister Hilaire was cured of chronic gastroenteritis on August 20, 1904. Sister Beatrix was cured of tuberculosis and laryngeal-bronchitis on August 31, 1904. Marie-Therese Noblet was healed of Pott's disease "of peculiar appearance, owing to some concomitant nervous phenomena" on August 31, 1905. Cecile Doubille de Franssu was restored to health on September 21, 1905 after being cured of tuberculous peritonitis. Antonia

Moulin suffered from an abscess of the right leg with phlebitis and lymphangitis; she was restored to health on August 8, 1907. Marie Borel was healed of abscesses, fistulas, and bowel obstructions on August 21, 1907. Virginie Haudebourg suffered from constant urinary infections, cystitis and nephritis. She was cured on May 17, 1908.

For the Catholic these are miracles; for a skeptical scientist these are unexplainable phenomena. An unbelieving scientist would argue that the human body is a complex and not fully understood reality capable of acting in ways that are often unexplainable to the mind. For such a person, something puzzling and contrary to the natural progress of a disease has occurred. Yet this puzzling, unexplainable, phenomenon cannot but make the unbeliever question: How did this occur? Are miracles possible? What is the cause of this mystery?

Reprising *Pascal's Wager*, whether miracles exist or not, it is to one's advantage to believe in them. Studies, too numerous to list, have shown that people who pray and believe in miracles tend to respond better to treatment, recover more quickly from surgery, and tend to overcome serious illnesses easier.

The existence of Lourdes is an argument that favors the existence of God.

FATIMA

The miracle of Fatima is one worth talking about since it was observed by atheists. On May 13, 1917 three young peasant children, Lucia dos Santos, Francisco Marto and his sister Jacinta saw a vision of Mary. On October 13, 1917, in the presence of an estimated crowd of 70,000 pilgrims, and in the presence of Communist newspaper writers, Mary appeared and then a "solar phenomena" appeared. A. Garrett, a professor at the University of Goimbra, explained the phenomena:

> *The sun, a few moments before, had pierced the thick clouds that held it hidden so that it shone clear and strongly. . . . It looked like a burnished wheel cut out of mother-o'-pearl. . . . The disc span dizzily round . . .: it whirled round upon itself with mad rapidity. . . . Then the sun, preserving the celerity of its rotation, detached itself from the firmament and advanced, blood-red, towards the earth, threatening to crush us with the weight of its vast and fiery mass.*[2]

The atheist, pro-government, anti-clerical Lisbon paper, *O Seculo*, wrote:

> *From the road, where the vehicles were parked and where hundreds of people who had not dared to brave the mud were congregated, one could see the im-*

mense multitude turn toward the sun, which appeared free from clouds and in its zenith. It looked like a plaque of dull silver, and it was possible to look at it without the least discomfort. It might have been an eclipse which was taking place. But at that moment a great shout went up, and one could hear the spectators nearest at hand shouting: 'A miracle! A miracle!' . . . Before the astonished eyes of the crowd . . . the sun trembled, made sudden incredible movements outside all cosmic laws—the sun 'danced' according to the typical expression of the people. People then began to ask each other what they had seen. The great majority admitted to having seen the trembling and the dancing of the sun; others swore that the sun whirled on itself like a giant Catherine wheel and that it lowered itself to the earth as if to burn it in its rays.

In the October 17, 1917 edition of the Lisbon paper, *O Dia*, we read:

At one o'clock in the afternoon, midday by the sun, the rain stopped. The sky, pearly grey in color, illuminated the vast arid landscape with a strange light. The sun had a transparent gauzy veil so that the eyes could easily be fixed upon it. The grey mother-of-pearl tone turned into a sheet of silver which broke up as the clouds were torn apart and the silver sun, enveloped in the same gauzy grey light, was seen to whirl and turn in the circle of broken clouds. A cry went up from every mouth and people fell on their knees on the muddy ground. . . . The light turned a beautiful blue, as if it had come through the stained-glass windows of a cathedral, and spread itself over the people who knelt with outstretched hands. The blue faded slowly, and then the light seemed to pass through yellow glass. Yellow stains fell against white handkerchiefs, against the dark skirts of the women. They were repeated on the trees, on the stones and on the serra. People wept and prayed with uncovered heads, in the presence of a miracle they had awaited. The seconds seemed like hours, so vivid were they.

From twenty-five miles away, the atheist (or more appropriately the former atheist) Alfonso Lopes Vieira commented: "On that day of October I was enchanted by a remarkable spectacle in the sky of a kind I had never seen before." *Mass hallucinations don't affect people living twenty-five miles away.*

The Blessed Mother predicted the Bolshevik Revolution and the spread of atheism and communism. She predicted World War II, and the name of the pope who would reign, and she predicted that Francisco and Jacinto would, shortly after the end of the apparitions, be taken up to heaven.

Unlike Nostradamus, whose writings can be interpreted in many ways, Fatima's predictions are so precise that they are not open to alternative interpretations! Difficult to believe? Read the accounts for yourself.

The events that took place in Portugal are either the most improbable examples of coincidences coming together or a truly miraculous series of events.

Miracles are not made to convert, but to make one ponder. If you are interested in miracles, with the advent of the internet, they are easy to find.

NOTES

1. The following are from the case files of the Medical Bureau of Lourdes.
2. C.C. Martindale, *The Message of Fatima* (New York: London, Burns and Oates, 1950), 77–78.

Argument from Providence

Coincidence is God's way of remaining anonymous.

Einstein

When we examine our lives, we see that there are no coincidences. What we view as chance or coincidence or synchronicity is in reality providence. God uses the ordinary and extraordinary circumstances of life to show us his presence.

There are so many examples from our personal lives and world history to affirm this point that I will simply focus on a few examples.

The priest Maximillian Kolbe was sent by the Nazis to the concentration camp at Auschwitz. His life would change the life of a complete stranger and in some ways the world. The *Oxford Dictionary of Saints* explains the circumstances surrounding Kolbe:

> *If anyone attempted to escape from the camp, men from the same bunker were selected for death by starvation. Near the end of July [1941], following an escape, men from Kolbe's bunker were paraded, knowing what to expect. One man from each line was selected including a sergeant, Francis Gajowniczek. When like the others he shouted out in despair, Kolbe stepped forward saying, "I am a Catholic priest. I wish to die for that man. I am old; he has a wife and children." The officer, keen to liquidate the old and the weak, changed numbers. Maximillian went to the death chamber of Cell 18. . . . [Two weeks later] he was injected with phenol and died on August 14.*[1]

Francis Gajowniczek promised God that if he survived Auschwitz, he would spend the rest of his life telling the story of what Kolbe did for him. He survived Auschwitz, and brought to the world the story of Maximillian Kolbe.

COINCIDENCE, CHANCE, SYNCHRONICITY, OR GOD'S PROVIDENCE?

A young priest, Karol Wojtyla, went to confession to the priest, stigmatist, and future saint, Padre Pio. He was told that he would one day become a pope. Karol became Pope John Paul II. *Coincidence, chance, synchronicity, or God's providence?*

Padre Pio had the stigmata, the wounds of Jesus in his hands and feet. He told his friars that after suffering for fifty years with these wounds, they would disappear, and then he would die. After fifty years the wounds disappeared, and Padre Pio died. *Coincidence, chance, synchronicity, or God's providence?*

On Good Friday, after the betrayal of Judas and the arrest of Jesus, the apostles ran away for fear of being captured and killed. Only the apostle John, Mary the Mother of Jesus, Mary Magdalene, and Mary the mother of James, Joses, and Salome had the strength to stand at the foot of the cross and see Jesus die. The apostles scattered, finally hiding in the 'upper room' fearing what would happen. Would they be captured? Would they be forgotten? What were they to do? Perhaps they hoped that all would just go away! Then something happened on Sunday that would forever change the lives of the apostles and the world. What was this something that happened? Scared apostles and disciples became suddenly courageous. Where once they ran, now they stood with dignity. Where once they hid, they now went to proclaim the Gospel on the rooftops to the whole world. James the Great, the son of Zebedee, evangelized Palestine and perhaps Spain. He was decapitated in 43 AD in Jerusalem. Matthias evangelized Palestine, Scythia, and Armenia. On his return to Jerusalem in 51 he was stoned to death by a mob of hostile Jews. Nathaniel (Bartholomew) evangelized Palestine, Asia Minor, Armenia, central India and Iran. He was flayed and crucified in Iran in 57 AD. James the Less, the son of Alphaeus, evangelized Palestine and was stoned to death by a mob in the year 60. Andrew evangelized Palestine, Asia Minor, Scythia, and Greece. He was crucified in Patras, Greece in the year 65. Simon bar Jonah, who would forever be known as Peter, the Rock, evangelized Palestine, Syria, Asia Minor and Rome. He was crucified upside down during the persecution of the emperor Nero and buried on Vatican Hill in the year 67 AD. Thomas evangelized Palestine, Osroene, Armenia, Egypt, and India. His great efforts in India earned him the title of "Apostle to the Indians." He was stabbed to death in the midst of a Hindu mob in Burma in 72 AD. Simon the Zealot evangelized Palestine, Egypt, North Africa, Britain, and Iran and Jude evangelized Palestine, Osroene, Armenia, and Iran. While Simon and Jude were in Iran, they were attacked by a mob led by pagan magi and were killed:

Simon being mutilated and sawed to pieces, and Jude being impaled by a spear. Both died in 79 AD. Matthew evangelized Palestine, Egypt, Ethiopia, and Iran. Philip evangelized Palestine, North Africa, and Asia Minor. He was crucified upside down in 87. It is unknown how Matthew died: some accounts have him as martyred and others have him as dying of natural causes in 90 AD. The apostle John was the last to die after evangelizing Palestine and Asia Minor. He died in exile in the year 100. His death marked the end of the apostolic age.

What can explain this change? History points to cult members who are willing to die for their *master*, but history also reveals that there are no accounts of cult followers willing to die for their cult leader some 60+ years later. The brainwashing of a cult leader quickly dwindles away when the influence or presence of the cult leader disappears.

So what explains the difference in the apostles? *Coincidence, chance, synchronicity?* What converted an anti-Christian Jew, Saul of Tarsus, to become Christianity's greatest evangelist? *Coincidence, chance, synchronicity? I prefer the resurrection of Christ!*

Jesus reminded his disciples that he would always be with his Church—and that the gates of hell would never prevail against it. Napoleon and Stalin were convinced they would wipe out Christianity from the face of the world. Both are dead, and the Church is still here!

A PERSONAL NOTE

I have used religious examples in my argument from providence. All of us, if we take time to reflect, know the providential. Any examination of history, secular or religious, bears the marks of God's providence.

As for me, I believe that I am a product of providence. I believe we are all a product of providence.

My mother, Florence, declared barren by doctors, was told by her uncle, a priest on his deathbed, that she would give birth to a child, that he would be born on the feast of Saint Joseph, and that he would be a priest. I am the only child of Florence and Renato, and I was born on the feast of Saint Joseph, and I am a priest. *Coincidence, chance, synchronicity, or God's providence?*

NOTE

1. *The Oxford Dictionary of the Saints*, ed. David Farmer (New York: Oxford University Press, 1987).

XII

Argument from
Spiritual Development[1]

According to the atheist co-discoverer of the DNA Double Helix, Francis Crick, and the Harvard cognitive scientist, Steve Pinker, our brains evolved for survival not for truth. Charles Darwin would wonder: "The horrid doubt always arises whether the conviction of man's mind, which has developed from the mind of the lower animals, is of any value or at all trustworthy. Would anyone trust the conviction of a monkey's mind, if there were any convictions in such a mind?"[2]

The fact that we can acquire truth means that we can experience the spiritual—which is nothing other than living in harmony with and in truth.[3] In other words, innate to the individual is the pull toward spiritual perfection, truth.

We are attracted to God by nature. It is for this reason that religions that acknowledge supernatural realities often share similar spiritual journeys.

There are universal wants that need to be met. All people desire renewal, forgiveness, community, peace, meaning, purpose, immortality, salvation, and a means for authentic living. Everyone needs a means to deal with the trials and tribulations of life. Everyone wants to make their joys more joyful and their times of difficulty easier to overcome. Because the world and people face similar challenges and desires, it is not unusual to see similarities.

The concept that religion makes man fully human is in direct conflict with atheist thought, as the words of Marx exemplify: "Man makes religion, religion does not make man."[4] The eternal truth of spiritual growth is a direct refutation of this paradigm.

God attracts us in many ways, but he does so in essentially four ways.

People are often awakened or attracted to God because God gives them a sense of meaning and purpose in life. One recognizes that one must be more than some complex organism that is born, lives, struggles, and dies in emptiness. Life in many ways would be a farce if that were so. Life would be inevitably on the edge of disintegration. No, there must be more to life than mere existence, than mere survival. Life needs purpose and meaning, a purpose and meaning that transcends the here and now. A life with purpose and meaning is a happy life. Despair is always associated to some degree with the loss of meaning and purpose.

Many are attracted to God because he is *Truth*. Such people seek truth in life, no matter where they may find it. Such people find great comfort in God for he is the goal of their quest, truth itself. Hence, life becomes for such individuals a delving into the mysteries of God, which consumes the entirety of their lives and gives them their ultimate joy.

Some people find God by seeing the good around them. The former atheist, Malcolm Muggeridge, a renowned reporter for the BBC, was such a person in many respects. It was in seeing the good that was in the heart of Mother Teresa of Calcutta that he was able to find Christ. In Mother Teresa he saw Jesus Christ, and his life would never be the same. God is good, and those who have found authentic goodness have found God.

Many are attracted to God because they see in the beauty of creation the handprint of God. For them all of creation echoes the beauty and providence of God. To find authentic beauty is to find the source of all beauty, God.

As one grows one develops a healthy balance between thinking and feeling, between grasping the transcendent and the immanent.

As one grows, one sees life's difficulties and sufferings as moments of purification and perfecting. The old self confronts a newer self. One's behaviors, beliefs, attitudes, and desires become reevaluated. Priorities are reordered. Moral integration begins. A movement from infantile faith and trust which are self-centered start to evolve into a faith that is other-centered. Sins or acts of disharmony—by omission or commission—are easily identified and begin to be conquered. A newer, better self evolves.

Pillars of growth begin to take hold. Humility—which is nothing other than self-knowledge in the presence of the transcendent—love, silence, a hunger for truth, and a desire to be detached of all so as to love all as all is meant to be loved develops. One begins to surrender and trust in that which is beyond the self.

Predominant faults and inclinations become illuminated. Alienation, anger, bitterness, meaningless, boredom, depression, an inability to get along with others, and other self destructive behaviors become illuminated and removed. One's blind sides become illuminated and eliminated.

Grace begins to build upon, heal, and elevate the nature of the person. Conscience becomes acute. The uninformed conscience—due to laziness and a sinful or disharmonious life—becomes informed and nourished through reflection, self-examination, and introspection. The hallmark of a well-informed conscience is identified: 1) A good end does not justify an evil means; 2) Do unto others as you would like done unto you.

As one progresses, one encounters a *darkness*. This is a time to choose: Do I go forward or do I allow myself to fall back? If one decides to move on, a dark night or deep spiritual cleansing takes place.

Vulnerability sets in. Prayer and the spiritual life seem dry, without consolation. One often feels rejected by family, friends, and society. Life can even seem to be falling apart. It is in this darkness that God is most active, purifying the imagination, memory, intellect, and will. One is beginning to experience God by means of the spirit as opposed to the senses. The lower forms of prayer such as petition and meditation are being transformed into the higher forms of prayer such as contemplation. One becomes aware of whether one is experiencing this *darkness* due to psychological problems—despair, illness—or through an authentic cleansing of the soul—marked by an unwavering faith, hope, and love amidst the trials and suffering.

This stage is a stage that most theists do not like to go through, and it is therefore the reason that most theists rarely move beyond this most simple level of the spiritual life. It is in these *believers in God* that atheists see nothing particularly extraordinary or significant.

For those who persevere into and through the *dark night*, illumination and enlightenment follows. It is at this stage that the flourishing of the virtues and the gifts of God come to fruition. The supernatural virtues of faith, hope, and love, and the cornerstone virtues of prudence, temperance, justice, and fortitude flourish. Pride, lust, unjustified anger, gluttony, envy, sloth, and inordinate cravings are slowly eradicated.

One begins to discern between the spirit of the world, the spirit of evil and the spirit of the divine.

The spirit of the world and evil is marked by pride, discouragement, despair, scrupulosity, boasting, dissension, hatred, false humility, presumption, fear of correction, self-infatuation, bitter zeal, lack of obedience, and an intense dislike for detachment and mortification. The person is pleasure oriented, self-oriented, easily irritated, easily discouraged, indifferent to the transcendental or anything beyond one's comprehension. They are people of tepidity, mediocrity, and false moderation.

The spirit of the divine is marked by faith, hope and love, a holy zeal, humility (self-knowledge), interior joy, forgetfulness of self, discretion, obedience, and the ability to embrace suffering. The world's standards of success or failure become irrelevant. This spiritual discernment is at the heart of spiritual growth and authentic *human-ness*.

Prayer at this level moves into the sphere of contemplation, from the prayer of quiet to the prayer of simple union, and finally to the prayer of transforming union (where the mystics enter into a spiritual betrothal and a spiritual marriage with the divine). Peace, quiet, calm, repose, serenity, and rest are the fruits of this experience. Knowledge of realities that transcend the natural means of knowing are infused. A deepening, wounding, inflaming, engulfing, inflowing, longing love for the divine and the desire to grow in the image and likeness of that which is loved, the divine, God, matures.

For the few that continue the journey, a final, intense purification is experienced, often referred to as the *passive purification of the soul*. An excess of God's presence blinds all the faculties of the person so as to purify all the faculties of the person. It is in this final purification that one is divested of the defects of the will, reasoning, memory, imagination, and prayer. One comes through this process a mystic! As St. Therese of Lisieux described the situation: "In the crucible of trails from within and without, my soul has been refined, and I can raise my head like a flower after a storm and see how the words of the Psalm have been fulfilled: 'The Lord is my Shepherd and there is nothing other that I shall need.'"

The mystical stage is marked by the living out of the heroic virtues and the spiritualization of the senses to heights beyond human capacities. It finds a beautiful expression in the prayer of St. Francis:

> *Lord, make me an instrument of your peace. Where there is hatred, let me sow love. Where there is injury, pardon. Where there is doubt, faith. Where there is despair, hope. Where there is darkness, light. Where there is sadness, joy. O Divine Master, grant that I not so much seek to be consoled as to console; to be understood as to understand; to be loved as to love. For it is in giving that we receive; it is in pardoning that we are pardoned; and it is in dying that we are born to eternal life.*

The fact that many throughout the world move from anxiety to peace, from meaninglessness to purpose and meaning, from bitterness or anger to love, from self-centeredness to other-centeredness, from doubt to faith, from despair to hope, from darkness to light, from disharmony to harmony, from disintegration to integration, from sadness to a taste of heaven is a sign of the universality of the experience of God. It is a journey that makes our joys more joyful and our times of sufferings easier to overcome.

The spiritual journey is another example of Pascal's Wager made valid!

God makes us function properly. Living without God causes disintegration. Therefore God exists!

NOTES

1. John Pasquini, *Light Happiness, and Peace* (New York: Alba House, 2004).

2. Charles Darwin, *On the Origin of Species*, 189.

3. Francis Crick, *The Astonishing Hypothesis: The Scientific Search for the Soul* (New York: Touchtone, 1995), 262; Steve Pinker, *How the Mind Works* (New York: Norton, 1997), 305. Given the evolutionary process, the experience of the transcendental is beneficial for the survival of the species as a whole. If God exists or does not, those who oppose a belief in God are hurting the species.

4. Karl Marx, *On Religion*, ed. and trans. Saul K. Padover (New York: McGraw Hill, 1974), 41.

XIII

Answered Prayers?

A young child lost his marble and began crying. When his father came home, the boy could not be consoled. His father turned to his son, took him by the hand and began praying. The boy prayed that he would find his marble. The next day, when the father came home from work, he asked, hesitantly, "My son, did you find your favorite marble?" The boy responded, *"No, dad, I didn't. But that's okay. God made me not want the marble anymore."* Prayer changes the prayer!

Atheists often argue against the belief in God because prayers are not provable objectively. The fact is that prayers are always answered, but not necessarily in the manner in which one expects prayers to be answered. Prayers are answered in such a fashion that one's eternal destiny, one salvation is always in the forefront. Prayer is always answered with the understanding that this earthly life is but a blink of the eye when compared to eternity. Prayer is always understood from the perspective of the present and future good of the world and with the understanding that all prayers are interconnected—at the level of the individual, the community, and the world.

When we look upon our prayers and desires, we see that our prayers were in fact answered, but most often in ways we did not expect. This is beautifully illustrated in the words of an unknown civil war soldier:

I asked for strength that I might achieve; I was made weak that I might learn humbly to obey. I asked for health that I might do greater things; I was given infirmity that I might do better things. I asked for riches that I might be happy; I was given poverty that I might be wise. I asked for power that I might have the praise of men; I was given weakness that I might feel the need of God. I asked for all things that I might enjoy life; I was given life that I might enjoy all things. I got nothing that I asked for, but everything that I had hoped for.

Almost despite myself, my unspoken prayers were answered; I am, among all men, most richly blessed.

Prayer is not the manipulating of God to acquire something that God did not know we needed; quite the contrary, God knows all, including our needs. We pray to show our need, our love, and our dependence upon him. It is in this act of love that God provides the means for our eternal life.

XIV

Argument from Disintegration

[Some animals expel] a wounded animal from the herd, or gore or worry it to death . . . [and this is the blackest part of natural selection].[1]
Charles Darwin

God exists because the world disintegrates when it represses his existence.
God exists because the world is "wired" for him!

Author

On Friday, April 8, 2005 Pope John Paul the Great was given the gift of the Mass of Resurrection, the Funeral Mass. For those who are familiar with funeral Masses you may have noticed something unique. The cardinals and priests were not dressed in white vestments, but red. How very appropriate! For John Paul II paid a heavy price, suffered much, even from his own Catholic flock, for proclaiming the Gospel of life, for combating the culture of death and promoting the culture of life. He was a true martyr for the cause. He so appropriately deserved the red vestment, the vestment of a martyr.

John Paul II reminded us of what the Sanhedrin's teacher of the law and the High Priest proclaimed after the resurrection of Jesus: "What is of God shall flourish. What is not of God shall die out and disintegrate. And beware of opposing what is of God for you may very well find yourself fighting God!"

Why are so many cultures dying and disintegrating? It is very simple: They are fighting God!

God exists because the world cannot function without him. A car without oil is a car whose engine will seize and cease to function. As oil is necessary for an engine, God is necessary for the world. God exists, because the world disintegrates when it represses his existence. God exists because the world is "wired" for him!

SECULARISM'S GREAT FAILURE

What has the growth of atheism done for the world? Has it brought the world and individuals closer to what atheists thought it would? Has secularism made things better? Daniel Dennett's claim that a belief in God is more harmful than good will be put to the test![2]

Any system of belief that does not recognize the transcendent is bound to leave a legacy of disintegration and debauchery. As Dostoevsky observed, "If God is dead then everything is permitted."[3]

The great failure of atheism is found in its naïve anthropology and its refusal to recognize the self-evident and what is often referred to as common sense. Atheism fails to recognize one's innate inclination toward the dysfunctional and one's innate inability to control one's future and one's surroundings. It falls short in recognizing the human person's natural inclination toward self-centeredness. It fails to recognize the demands of or even the existence of the natural law and the existence of absolutes such as truth.

The rise of atheism has not brought about its hoped for freedom or personal autonomy or utopia. Instead, it has brought about the enslavement of societies to their passions, desires, and dysfunctions. It has brought about a revival of paganism, barbarism, and anarchy.

Belief in God has always been a restraining force to the intrinsic evil inclinations within the human person: The abandoning of God in our modern culture has brought about the unshackling of restraints. Atheism is birthing an unrestrained culture that inevitably will become a den of thieves, murderers, gluttons, and perverts.

The future looks bleak. The last levee is about to breach, if we do not make radical changes. The only thing holding back atheism's complete victory into debauchery is the use of criminal laws and the doctrine of political correctness. But even this is about to collapse under the ever increasing waves of nominalism, pragmaticism, hedonism, positivism, and relativism.

Without absolutes as a levee of protection, a society flushes out whatever good it has. When everything is based on usefulness, self-preservation, hedonism, consensus, the survival of the fittest, then a culture disintegrates. The debauchery of yesteryear becomes the acceptable practice of today. In the past, contraception, abortion, euthanasia, homosexual activity, and divorce were considered unmentionables. Today these unmentionables have become perfectly acceptable. They have become politically correct.

Atheism, by nature, leads to the death of a culture. It leads to a pagan, barbaric, anarchistic culture. Just as the lives of the world's most famous atheists have left a legacy of anger, bitterness, despair, and moral and mental collapse, so too will the cultures that they sought to build: Nietzsche, the *god of atheism*, the *superman*, became a bumbling, broken down wreck. The society he sought to foster, and which has come about to a great degree, will also become a bumbling, broken down wreck if we do not wake up from our slumber—if we do not see through the atheist delusion.

When we look at the atrocities of history, nothing equals the atrocities done by atheists.

The atheists Nietzsche and Schopenhauer formed the very foundation and structural framework for Nazi Germany, for Hitler's Teutonic religion. The atheistic Soviet Union through mass executions, warfare, imposed starvation and forced labor destroyed millions upon millions of individuals. Statistics point to the fact that six to eight million people were killed under Lenin, twenty to twenty-five under Stalin. Eastern Europe, under Soviet rule, accounts for at least two to three million deaths in the name of communism. Mao's China equals in terms of carnage that of the Soviet Union.

The statesman Zbigniew Brzezinski wrote in his work *Out of Control* that over sixty million lives were lost during the reign of atheism in the communist world, making, as he stated, "atheistic communism the most costly experiment and failure in human history."[4]

The belief in that which transcends oneself is the only factor that can keep a person and a culture from disintegrating—for the belief in that which transcends oneself is the only thing that can keep one answerable to something other than oneself or *one's fellow man*!

A Distorted Utopian Love

The failure made by atheists, and consequently the source of much of its evils, is its distorted concept of love. Atheists, such as Feuerbach, see love as that which is universal and inclusive. Love is universal, but is not necessarily inclusive. Unconditional acceptance is not equivalent to unconditional love!

Let us look at the atheist utopia.

PERSONHOOD

Atheism is no admirer of persons, despite its superficial claims. Atheism's value for the person is based on the *survival of the fittest* mentality, on a dog eat dog world, on a use up and throw away mentality.

If you were to ask any embryologist when life begins, you would hear without hesitation: "Life begins when a human ovum is fertilized by a human spermatozoa. That is, life begins at syngamy when a one-celled zygote is produced. At syngamy a human organism, a member of the human species, comes into existence." In other words, in terms we can understand, human life begins at conception (syngamy).[5]

At conception we have a human organism, a human being. We do not have a baboon organism or a chimpanzee organism or an elephant organism.

Having said this, however, one may ask: "If this is so, why is it that abortion, stem cell research on embryos, artificial reproduction and all kinds of experimentations on embryos is permitted to take place?"

There are many reasons, as we shall see further on. But one of the main reasons comes from an ancient pagan theory that is often today referred to as the *theory of delayed hominization*. This theory essentially maintains that one can be a human organism without being a human person. Therefore, if one is not a human person then one does not have the rights of a human person.

The great dilemma that arises from such a view is: When does one become a person? For some individuals, one becomes a person at approximately two weeks after conception when the embryo is implanted in the uterus; for others it is at three weeks when the heart is beating, or at six weeks when brain waves are measurable and the child moves and responds to touch, or at eight weeks when the body is completely formed, or at twelve weeks when all organ systems are functioning, or at twenty weeks at viability (when the child can live outside the womb), or at birth, or at infancy, or at four to six years of age. That's right—birth, infancy, and four to six years of age.

Some scientists argue that if a child is born with a defect, then a mother should have the right to euthanize (kill) the child within the first two to three days of birth.[6] The so-called scholar Tristram Engelhardt Jr. maintains that one is not a human person until one is able to experience abstract thought and reflective self-consciousness.[7]

Does this remind you of anything? This hideous and false portrayal of life has tragic consequences, for if one can assign personhood by an arbitrary standard, then one can take away *personhood* accordingly by an arbitrary standard.

In the early years of this country, slavery was justified on the grounds that slaves were considered property and not persons. In Nazi Germany the handicapped, the seriously ill, the gypsies, and finally the Jews and all who opposed Nazism were exterminated for failing to be authentic Aryan persons. As the Nazis would say of the handicapped World War I veterans before they were exterminated: "These are useless eaters."

If you take a person's personhood away, you can do almost anything to a person. When one plays with a person's personhood all kinds of egregious acts are in the shadows waiting to come out.

Since many Alzheimer's patients and many mentally handicapped individuals are incapable of abstract thought and self-reflection, are they to be put to death for not being persons?

Logic dictates that one is a human being and a human person from the moment of conception. There is no separating of the two! As Pope John Paul II clarified in the *Gospel of Life*: "How can one be a human being without being a human person?" Or as the ecclesiastical writer of the third century, Tertullian, wrote: "One becomes a human person only because one already is a human person."

At the moment of conception a person's sex, facial features, body type, hair, eye, and skin color are determined. Even a person's future intelligence and personality are influenced by the genetic code present at conception. Every aspect of who and what a person is is present from the beginning of human life with the exception of the exercise of free will, time to grow and mature, and the influences of the environment. What I am at 44 is what I was at conception with the exception of the exercise of my will, time to grow and mature, and environmental influences. Everything I will be at 67 is what I am now at 44, with the same exceptions.

From the moment of conception, we are simultaneously human beings and human persons. Once this image is suppressed, however, the secular view of the person takes over, and once this occurs, the disintegration of a society is close by.

With the secular denial of absolutes, essences, universals, and objective truth comes a science infected with the opinions, consensuses, preferences, emotions, psychological attitudes and social pressures of the time. A person's usefulness to society becomes the only valid criterion for personhood.

The atheistic concept of the human person leads to atrocities. *God exists because the world disintegrates when it represses his existence. God exists because the world is "wired" for him!*

CONTRACEPTION[8]

A life based on subjective, personal, and temporal perceptions, on nominalistic, pragmatic, egoistic, positivistic, evolutionistic, relativistic conceptions of reality is a life that loses its essence of meaning and opens the door to moral decay. When the natural law, the natural order of things is denied, when absolutes and objective truths are denied or made irrelevant, then evil prevails.

If we were to ask most couples about the negative side effects associated with the use of the pill, most couples would have a general idea regarding these effects, either through information obtained from their doctors or from pharmacists. They may not be aware of the fifty-two side effects associated with the use of the pill, but they more than likely would be aware of the most talked about side effects such as strokes, heart attacks, and blood clots.

If, however, we were to ask most couples about the method in which the pill works in preventing the birth of children, there would be a tremendous amount of ignorance.

There are two major types of pills that are being used in preventing the birth of children: those that contain a combination of estrogen and progestogen and those that contain only progestogen. Both of these types of pills prevent the birth of children either through preventing ovulation or preventing the effective migration of sperm in the uterus, or by preventing implantation.

In the *Physicians' Desk Reference* the combination pills are described as operating in the following manner: "Combination oral contraceptives act by suppression of gonadotropins. Although the primary mechanism of this action is the inhibition of ovulation, other alterations include changes in the cervical mucus (which increase the difficulty of sperm entry into the uterus) and the endometrium (which reduces the likelihood of implantation)."

In terms of the progestogen-only pill, the *Physicians' Desk Reference* states: "[Progestogen-only pills] alter cervical mucus, exert a progestational effect on the endometrium, interfering with implantation, and in some patients, suppress ovulation."

Therefore, the pill (whether the combination pill or the progestogen-only pill) has the potential for being an abortifacient—an abortion-causing agent. When conception takes place, a human being is present. The pill at this point, because it weakens the lining of the uterus, prevents this human being from being implanted in the womb of the mother.

This is a silent abortion. As the Catholic Church teaches in its documents, and in particular in the 1994 American document *Ethical and Religious Directives for Catholic Health Care Services* (n. 45): "Every procedure whose sole immediate effect is the termination of pregnancy before viability is an abortion, which, in its moral context, includes the interval between conception and implantation of the embryo."

What is said of the *pill* can be said, with slight variations, of all the other hormonal methods of contraception including Norplant, Depo-Provera, RU-486 and Ovral.

Similar abortifacient effects are also apparent in the use of intrauterine devices such as Lippes Loop and the Copper-T 380A.

How many silent victims are being lost because of the unknowing actions of couples? Who is at fault for their ignorance? What kinds of philosophies have produced the dummying down of a culture that allows for such atrocities to take place?

Life based on subjective, personal, and temporal perceptions, on nominal-istic, pragmatic, egoistic, hedonistic, positivistic, evolutionistic, relativistic conceptions is a life that loses its essence of meaning, its respect for the natural order of creation, and opens the door to the disintegration and dummying down of a culture.

Contraception has led to a contraceptive, use up and throw-away mentality in our society. Divorce is almost the norm; promiscuity is safeguarded from unwed pregnancies, sex is hedonistic, people are sex tools, sex objects, or masturbatory tools of selfishness, self-centeredness, and self-interest.

Love is lost in contraception. The person, at best, can only say, "I love you, but only so much—not enough to spend my life with you or to have children with you." This is not love! People with this contraceptive mentality use people until their usefulness is no longer needed. Then they move on to the next empty experience.

Is it any wonder that the divorce rate of those who use contraceptives is fifty percent while the divorce rate of those who respect the natural order of their bodies in the unitive bond of committed monogamy, of marriage, is less than four percent?

In the use of contraceptives, the relationship between womanhood, mother-hood, sexuality and procreation is lost. What flows is a culture of divorce, promiscuity, and hatred for and the objectification of women and their procreative gifts. The contraceptive mentality destroys the bond between husband and wife, which in turn destroys the bond between children and parents, which in turn destroys the bond between children and God. Atheists, serial killers, and criminals of all sorts can trace their origins to this contraceptive mentality, this mentality that has distorted the relationship between woman-hood, motherhood, sexuality and procreation.

God exists because the world disintegrates when it represses his existence. God exists because the world is "wired" for him!

ABORTION[9]

One out of four children conceived in the United States is aborted, one every twenty-two seconds! Ninety-three percent of women regret their abortions!

The legalization of abortion has impacted and threatened the very structure of our society. Abortion is at the heart of much of the disintegration and de-bauchery we are experiencing in our times and will continue to experience.

The United States has anywhere between 3,600 to 4,500 abortions a day. And since its legalization in the early 1970's over forty million abortions have occurred. At approximately seven weeks of pregnancy, when the heart, brain, stomach, liver, and kidney are functioning, approximately 800,000 infants are aborted each year. At sixteen weeks when the child's organs are complete and functioning and the child is breathing (fluid), swallowing, digesting, sleeping, dreaming, and experiencing pleasure and pain, approximately 71,000 American babies are aborted each year.[10]

First-trimester aborted babies are disposed of by flushing them down a garbage disposal or *insinkerator*, or disposed of in biological waste bags. Larger bodies are often sold for research purposes. Third-trimester babies are often disposed of in on-site crematoria. In the most egregious cases, full-term babies have been burned alongside of dogs, cats, and birds and thrown out by local humane society offices. Some have even gone so far as to use meat grinders and garbage disposals.[11]

Abortion is the number one killer of Americans. One out of four infants conceived is aborted each day, one every twenty-two seconds. Forty-five abortions a day are performed on women in America who are five months or more into their pregnancy. Forty-three percent of women who have abortions will have two or more. While the average abortion takes five to ten minutes, the average wait to adopt a child is two to ten years.

In the World Trade Center terrorist attack, some 3,000 individuals died. This led to a war against terrorism and a war in Afghanistan and Iraq. Some 3,600 to 4,500 abortions take place every day in this country. Why are we not as outraged at these abortions as we were at the World Trade Center catastrophe? Why are we not as determined to put an end to abortion as we are to terrorism?

During the 2008 Presidential Race, a woman was seen holding a sign, "Stop the war on Iraq." A man standing next to her had a sign, "Stop the war on children in America." Approximately 3,500 soldiers have died in Iraq after six years of war. This is less than one day of abortions in the United States!

People are often more interested in voting for abortion promoting candidates out of a sense of preserving and getting more of what they already have! Four thousand dead children for a few pennies on the dollar! This can only happen in a secular society where self-preservation, good living, and self-pleasuring is god.

The total number of Americans who have been killed in American wars in the name of freedom and dignity is 1,178,863 (Revolutionary War, 25,324; War of 1812, 2,260; Mexican War, 13,283; Civil War, 498,332; Spanish-American War, 2,446; WWI, 116,708; WWII, 407,316; Korean War, 54,246; Vietnam War, 58,655; Persian Gulf War I, 293; Persian Gulf War II, 3,500/still undetermined).

Why have we failed to give the same dignity and freedom to forty million aborted children that we have sought, sacrificed, and fought to give to others? An atheist infected world that concerns itself with pleasure at all cost, avoiding suffering at all cost, on doing what is useful for one's self-interests is a society that can abort children. A society where majority opinion, social pressure, emotions, and preferences determine actions is a society where abortion is allowed to flourish. Such a society seeks to hide and manipulate the culture from that which it denies even exists, objective truth.

God exists because the world disintegrates when it represses his existence. God exists because the world is "wired" for him!

POST ABORTION TRAUMA—THE DAMAGING OF WOMEN

Trauma, if not dealt with, will manifest itself in the most negative of ways. Hence, the trauma of abortion, if not dealt with, will wreak havoc on a woman and consequently on much of society.

Women who have had abortions often seek to deal with the pain in essentially four manners: through suppression, repression, rationalization, and/or compensation.[12]

Suppression

Women who seek to suppress the trauma of abortion consciously push away or push down any negative feelings. They do everything possible not to think about the abortion or its trauma. These are women who often turn to alcohol or drugs to numb their pain, or become workaholics to keep busy and distracted, or avoid prayer, church, and God. It is not unusual to notice a person get up and walk out of church when the very word abortion is mentioned. They are not being disrespectful. They are simply avoiding a reminder of their trauma.

In the most extreme cases, women who suppress their pain will often have more than one abortion (three to ten is not unusual) with the hope that each abortion will lessen the trauma (forty-five percent of women who have had an abortion, will have more than one). The mentality is: "The more I have, the less it will hurt."

Repression

Women who repress the trauma of abortion do so without any conscious awareness. Repression is a subconscious defense mechanism where the mind blocks out any negativity. These repressed feelings manifest themselves through an inability to bond with their husbands or children and an inability to form deep relationships.

Repression also manifests itself in certain disorders and unexplained actions. A woman went in for counseling because of a lingering depression. The woman was astonishingly beautiful with the exception of her hair. It was so short that a comb could not pass through it. After months of therapy, the mystery was uncovered. The woman's hair was so short because she could not bear to hear the sound of a hair dryer. It reminded her of the suction catheter used during her abortion. Likewise, through therapy, another woman was able to recognize that the only reason she had replaced all her carpets in her home with wood flooring, was that the sound of the vacuum cleaner reminded her of the suction catheter used in her abortion. These women were doing things they could not explain because they were subconsciously trying to deal with the trauma of abortion. It was through therapy that what was being repressed came to light.

Rationalization

At a local abortion facility (while a group of pro-life individuals were gently and lovingly praying the rosary) a woman volunteer from the clinic drove into the parking lot, jumped out of her car, and ran over to confront a woman praying. She was so filled with anger and malice that her body shook as she screamed.

This is a classic example of the coping mechanism of rationalization at work. Rationalization is an argument that one makes to justify one's action as acceptable. It is marked by intolerance, anger, and hatred. If I were a betting man, I would bet that this volunteer had had an abortion at some time in her life, for many abortion facility workers are individuals who have had or participated in abortions.

The rationalization of many women who have had an abortion is that "if it is legal, it must be Okay." Any threat to the legal status of abortion is a threat to their coping with the trauma.

This is the same rationalization that is behind the efforts to eliminate the *Choose Life* plates in many states. These plates are a threat to the legal status of abortion.

Compensation

Compensation is a coping mechanism that seeks to *make up* for past mistakes. Often women feel they must be punished in order to compensate for the evil of their abortion. This manifests itself in self-mutilation, suicide, anorexia, bulimia, and a wide range of self-punishing behaviors.

This compensation mechanism is often seen in what is known as the *perfect mother syndrome*. Mothers often try to make up for what they did to their first child by trying to be the perfect mother for their subsequent children.

They can often become doting and controlling parents in their efforts to make everything perfect.

Let us make no mistake about it. Those who support abortion have no love for women.

In the name of the religion of atheism, women, families, and therefore the world is being harmed.

The destruction of women leads to the destruction of future generations of women and families. As families are damaged, atheism flourishes, for it is hard to see the handprint of a Triune God when the image of the Triune God cannot be seen imaged in the family.

Abortion is an *atheist cancer* that eats up societies; it is a poison that saps out any sense of compassion in a society.

POST ABORTION TRAUMA—A FAMILY WOUND

Women, Mothers

The trauma that women experience after having had an abortion takes on many forms and may appear immediately after the abortion or some forty years afterwards. One way or another, a woman's life will never be the same, either at a very conscious level or a subconscious level.

As discussed before, women who have had an abortion experience overwhelming feelings of guilt, isolation, grief, anger, depression, and shame. They often develop obsessive compulsive disorders and various forms of addictive behaviors such as eating disorders, and alcohol and drug abuse. Women often feel alienated from God and from their faith community. At times they feel anger at God and a sense that they can never be forgiven. They exhibit a hindered ability to bond with future children and their spouses. They often turn to atheism.

Men, Fathers

Men are often haunted by nightmares about their unborn children. They often develop feelings of great guilt, remorse, sadness, and powerlessness. They often punish themselves by forms of self abuse such as alcoholism, drug use, or bodily mutilations (i.e., extensive piercings and tattoos). At times men can turn feelings of betrayal, powerlessness, and loss of trust into acts of aggression and abuse toward women. Men often seek to run away from these feelings by leaving their partners. It is not unusual that an abortion marks the end of a relationship. This in turn helps to foster atheism, for one of the major causes of atheism is the absent father. More abortions, more atheism.

Siblings

Siblings are often afflicted by despair, confusion, and a general fear of the world. Because of repressed or subconscious anger, children of mothers who have had abortions have a higher rate of being physically abused. Siblings often suffer what is known as *Survivor Syndrome*, which is a mixture of anger and guilt associated with the overwhelming feeling of "why did I survive and my brother or sister didn't?" At times siblings feel that somehow their existence has caused the death of their sibling: "Mom and Dad could only handle one of us!" And in some cases children develop a paralyzing fear of their mothers, for they feel that "I might be next to get rid of." This too leads to a child predisposed to atheism, for the parental figure fails to image God.

Grandparents

Grandparents often experience many of the above symptoms of post-abortion trauma, but most feel a sense of anger, bitterness, resentment, depression and despair over the abortion. Often they feel unable to forgive their daughter or step-daughter. Most often, whether at a conscious or subconscious level, grandparents experience a strained relationship with their daughter or step-daughter.

Abortion is a family tragedy and a societal tragedy. The more we permit the continuance of abortion, the more the family will die out. When the family structure dies, cultures die, and societies die. Atheism is the vestige of dying and dead cultures and societies.

The growth of abortion on demand—birthed on secular philosophy—has put more than anything or anyone the *dysfunctional* into the dysfunctional family. When bonds are damaged between spouses, between parents and children, then crime increases and abuses of all sorts thrive. Society begins to disintegrate.

God exists because the world disintegrates when it represses his existence. God exists because the world is "wired" for him!

MODERN COMPREHENSIVE SEX EDUCATION—AN OUTGROWTH OF THE CONTRACEPTIVE MENTALITY AND ABORTION[13]

The sex education that I stand for . . . should automatically serve to bring home to children the essential distinction between man and brute, to make them realize that it is man's special privilege and pride to be gifted with the faculties of head and heart both, that he is a thinking no less than feeling animal, and to renounce the sovereignty of reason over the blind instincts is, therefore, to renounce a man's estate. In man, reason quickens and guides the feeling; in brutes, the soul lies ever dormant.[14]

Gandhi

The sex education programs found in schools today have left the world a legacy of sexual brutes, fostering large masses of individuals, if not entire generations, incapable of authentically loving.

There are essentially three types of sex education programs competing for acceptance in our culture. One is referred to as chastity education, another as biological sex education, and a final as comprehensive sex education.

Atheism, which has no concept for authentically understanding the essence of sexuality, has no place for chastity education. A culture that sees people as objects to be used for pleasure has no place for chastity. In a society where preference, emotion, and social acceptability determine what is right and wrong, chastity education becomes archaic. Hedonism, paganism, heathenism and debauchery are the natural consequence of an atheistic vision of sex.

Chastity Sex Education[15]

Chastity sex education is that which recognizes the uniqueness of individuals and fosters authentic sexual integrity and authentic love. It fosters self-mastery and integration in the most intimate dimension of the human person. It is only through chastity sex education that one can experience real love and the gifts that flow from fidelity. The reality is that one either controls one's sexual drive or one is controlled by it. As the 1995 Catholic document *The Truth and* Meaning of Human Sexuality states:

If the person is not the master of self—through the virtues and, in a concrete way, through chastity—he or she lacks that self-possession which makes self-giving possible. Chastity is the spiritual power which frees love from selfishness and aggression... Chastity is the joyous affirmation of someone who knows how to live a self-giving, free from any form of self-centered slavery, [life] ... Either man governs his passions and finds peace, or he lets himself be dominated by them and becomes unhappy.[16]

Chastity is not to be understood as a repressive attitude. On the contrary, chastity should be understood rather as the purity and temporary stewardship of a precious and rich gift of love, in view of the self-giving realized in each person's specific vocation. Chastity is thus the spiritual energy capable of defending love from the perils of selfishness and aggressiveness, and is able to advance it toward its full realization.[17]

Those who cannot master chastity will never be able to master fidelity and authentic self-giving for they will be slaves to their passions. They will never grasp the meaning of authentic family life, of authentic love and virtue and the respect for the innate gift of sexuality and life. They will never be able to understand the intrinsic spirituality of the sex act. The correlation between the rise of atheism and sex addiction is not coincidental.

The consequences of failing to foster chastity and self-mastery is the relinquishing of one's sexual energies to one's uncontrolled passions. This leads to the use of contraceptives (including abortifacients), divorce, abortion, child abuse, and distorted behaviors of all kinds. It leads to the disintegration between the body and soul, the physical and the spiritual. It leads to all forms of self-abuse, including the ever growing epidemic of suicide.

Comprehensive Sex Education

Atheists, and particularly those whose philosophical tendencies are toward the philosophies of atheistic evolutionism, pragmaticism, positivism and hedonism, see sex as simply a biological compulsion whose approval or disapproval is based on relativism, on what is socially acceptable or is in accordance with majority opinion or consensus opinion. Schools have indoctrinated whole generations of children to this view of life. If there are any doubts, turn on the television.

Building upon the purely biological, the comprehensive sex education program's philosophy is essentially as follows: "If it is between two consenting adults, it is acceptable." There is no right or wrong. There is no moral value system. There is no spiritual dimension to the person. There is no interest in interpersonal relationships or chastity skills. The person is an organism, like any other. One is an animal like any other, and thus one can for all practical purposes act like any other animal.

This is the philosophy that has conquered our culture and our school systems. And so what do the public school textbooks teach? Premarital sex, open marriages or free unions, group sex, homosexuality, bisexuality, sado-masochism, incest, bestiality, masturbation, sex with inanimate objects, etc., are all discussed without any moral significance. Birth control, abortion, sterilization, and so forth, are discussed without any value attached to them.

This philosophy says, "No sex act is immoral." It says, "No lifestyle must be judged."

What has this philosophy done to our culture? Since the sexual revolution of the 1960's what has atheism given us?[18] (Statistics since the 1960's):

- Despite the pushing of contraceptives, abortions have increased from 200,000 to 1.4 million per year.
- Cohabitation has increased from 500,000 to 4 million—cohabitation is more popular and common than marriage in the United States.
- Divorce has increased from 400,000 to 1.2 million per year.
- Single-parent families have risen from 9 to 32 percent.
- Illegitimate births have increased from 200,000 to 1.5 million per year.
- Teenage pregnancy has increased from 30 to 110 per 1000 girls annually.
- Sexually transmitted diseases have increased 245 percent.
- Child abuse has increased 286 percent.
- Crime rates have increased by 510 percent.

When sex is divorced from its spiritual dimension, it lowers the person to the level of a brute, an animal. One either controls one's sexual drive or one is controlled by it!

Is it any wonder that Christendom is no more? Is it any wonder that secularism, paganism or heathenism is on the rise?

God exists because the world disintegrates when it represses his existence. God exists because the world is "wired" for him!

PORNOGRAPHIC SOCIETY[19]

[Our objective is] unlimited sexual gratification without the burden of unwanted children . . . [Women must have the right] to live . . . to love . . . to be lazy . . . to be an unmarried mother . . . to create . . . to destroy . . . The marriage bed is the most degenerate influence in the social order . . . The most merciful thing that a family does to one of its infant members is to kill it"[20]

Margaret Sanger

The misuse of sexuality is one of the most detrimental dimensions of the religion of secularism, of atheism—and this is exemplified in a pornography infested society. Pornography is society's number one money making industry. It is sold everywhere, seen everywhere, and is thriving in leaps and bounds as the world goes deeper into the empty abyss of secularism.

The internet pornography industry generates more money than ABC, NBC, and CBS combined! The total porn industry has an estimated profit of four to ten billion dollars. Ninety percent of children between eight and sixteen have seen online pornography. The largest group of viewers of internet pornography are children between twelve and seventeen. It is estimated that ten to forty-five percent of Americans are addicted to pornography.[21]

Sex in this secular perspective is seen in terms of self-pleasuring and usefulness. It is devoid of all spiritual purpose and is completely alien to the very nature of conjugal love and the nature of the person. A person's sexuality in this atheistic perception of things has been distorted by the secular philosophies of pragmaticism, egoism, hedonism, positivism, and relativism.

A Catholic document titled *Human Sexuality* poignantly explains the damage that this secular pornographic contaminated society inflicts on individuals, marriages, children, and society in general.

> *Pornography, the use of visual or print media to present nudity and sexual activity in a degrading or depersonalizing way, often preys upon the most vulnerable in our society. Women, children, and men all too often are portrayed as objects at the disposal of the sexual lust or violent actions of others. Children, too, can find ready access to materials that may warp their view of women and men, of sexuality, and of the mutual love and responsibility that rightly ought to accompany sexual intimacy.*[22]

Pornography distorts the purpose of sexuality and affronts human dignity. It eliminates from the essence of sex the mutual vulnerability that makes human intimacy possible. Pornography replaces vulnerability for control, power, and the objectification of the person. Pornography makes a mockery of the rights of spouses, of the institution of marriage, and compromises the welfare of children who need a healthy two parent home for stability. Pornography is born from atheism and gives rise to more atheism.

Is it any wonder that adultery and marital infidelity are at epidemic levels? Is it any wonder that promiscuity has reached levels unheard of since the time of paganism? Is there any wonder that prostitution is rampant and has even gained a sense of legitimacy? Is it any wonder that a study by Neil Malamuth of UCLA reported that fifty percent of men would have no problem raping a woman if they could be assured of getting away with it?[23] Is it any wonder that ten year olds are sexually active and that twelve year olds are getting pregnant and having abortions? Is it any wonder that once the *spice of sex* is lost in a marriage, the marriage ends? Is it any wonder that rape, sexual assaults and child abuse have reached epidemic proportions?

When one debases oneself to the level of a brute animal, one cannot but act like a brute animal! Atheism is the religion of the brute!

God exists because the world disintegrates when it represses his existence. God exists because the world is "wired" for him!

CHILD ABUSE—THE RESULT OF THE DENIGRATION OF PERSONHOOD AND THE FAMILY

A contraceptive society, a society that accepts abortion as legal, a society where sex has lost its innate meaning is a society which opens itself to even more atrocities.

A life based on subjective, personal, and temporal perceptions, on nominalistic, pragmatic, egoistic, hedonistic, positivistic, evolutionistic, relativistic conceptions is a life that opens the door to atrocities.

Atheism, whose origins are founded in part in pragmaticism and relativism, opens the door to all forms of abuse, for when a person is not seen in terms of his or her essence that person becomes nothing more than an object. When pragmaticism and relativism infects a society then the image of the person as a useable, throw-away object of perversion becomes justifiable in the minds of the infected. One should not therefore be shocked at the epidemic growth of child abuse.

Society is wounded by an unimaginable number of individuals walking around who are suffering from various forms of pathological disorders due to such abuse.

Four children die every day in the United States from child abuse, three out of four before the age of four. An estimated 906,000 children are victims of abuse, 12.3 children per 1,000 children. A report of child abuse is made every ten seconds. Eighty percent of abused children develop a psychological disorder by the age of twenty-one—including depression, anxiety disorders, and post-traumatic stress disorder. Abused children are twenty-five percent more likely to have a childhood pregnancy. Fifty-nine percent are more likely to be arrested as a juvenile, twenty-eight percent as an adult. Thirty-six percent of all women and fourteen percent of all men in prison were abused as children. Abused children have a higher rate of alcohol and drug abuse. Two-thirds of all people in drug treatment programs report childhood abuse. One third of abused children will end up abusing their own children.[24]

One out of four girls and one out of seven boys will be sexually abused before the age of eighteen.

When the dignity or essence of the person is not taken seriously then evil is bound to follow. When relativistic, hedonistic, atheistic philosophies infect *God-believers* and *non-believers*, then personal preferences, emotions, desires, and even pathological needs become the source of justification for atrocities.

The abortion and contraceptive mentalities have led to a culture where abortion-damaged parents are unable to effectively bond with their children and children are unable to effectively bond with their parents. Abortion and contraception have led to the growth of repressed anger in families and a sense of alienation. This has given rise to a world of damaged people, a world twirling out of control, a world damaged by people suffering from the personality disorder of atheism.

The abortion and contraceptive mentalities have distorted the very nature of sex and therefore opened the door to decadence. And why should people be amazed at these atrocities when atheism's obsession with the self, with selfishness, and with its slavery to one's passions is the norm.

Atheism fosters atheism!

God exists because the world disintegrates when it represses his existence. God exists because the world is "wired" for him!

NO PLACE FOR THE POOR IN SECULARISM[25]

It is a poverty to decide that a child must die so that you may live as you wish.

Blessed Mother Teresa of Calcutta

What Blessed Mother Teresa said about abortion can very well be said about the hungry, the poor and the homeless around the world. If people cannot be respected at the beginning of life, why should they be at other stages of life?

It is so easy for us to harden our hearts to the plight of the less fortunate. Yet the Gospel and the *Catechism of the Catholic Church* continues to remind us of the need to love our neighbor, and to have a preferential option or love for the poor.[26] This is in complete contradiction to a society that worships the survival of the fittest and the useful. This is in complete contradiction to a society that is incapable of seeing a person beyond his or her biological functions. This is in complete contradiction to a society that denies the existence of the supernatural and the transcendental.

Nine hundred twenty-three million people across the world are hungry every day. Almost 16,000 children die of hunger every day, one every five seconds. Almost 1.4 billion people live below the $1.25 a day poverty line. Eight hundred and twenty million people are undernourished. Poor nutrition causes one in three to die prematurely. In 2006, 9.7 million children died before their first birthday due to poor nutrition. Most children die of complications due to diarrhea, respiratory illness, malaria and measles. Every year, twenty million low-birth weight babies are born.[27]

Helping the needy is not as much an act of charity as it is a demand for justice. As the Church Father John Chrysostom explained: "Not to enable the needy to share in our goods is to steal from them and deprive them of life."[28] Blessings are to be shared. In atheism's *dog eat dog* world, in secularism's pleasure and preference oriented world where selfishness, self-centeredness, and the avoidance of pain and suffering at all costs is promoted, where the cult of the body is the new practice of worship, the plight of the poor and disenfranchised is irrelevant.

The natural order of things demands of us that we build a world where a solidarity of nations can be established to eliminate hunger, poverty, and homelessness. It demands of us that we aid in the moral, cultural, and economic development of countries. This is a grave and unavoidable responsibility for the wealthiest nations. As the Christian Scriptures explain: "How can God's love survive in a man who has enough of this world's goods yet closes his heart to his brother when he sees him in need" (1 Jn. 3:17)?

Atheism has promoted class and caste systems and an unwillingness to lower one's standard of living for the good of others. This can only lead to an increasing warfare among the rich and the poor.

What little atheists do for the needy is virtually always done for self-aggrandizement, self-promotion, out of an innate, unconscious desire for some form of immortality. Put my name on it, and I'll donate! Send some money to them, or they'll bring their revolution upon us! Atheists give less to charity than any group in the world.

God exists because the world disintegrates when it represses his existence. God exists because the world is "wired" for him!

OVERPOPULATION—A MYTH PROMOTED BY HEDONISTIC SECULARISTS[29]

The idea that the world is overpopulated is a myth that the wealthy nations of the world and those with pro-abortion and pro-contraceptive agendas seek to promote. The wealthy nations seek to keep their standards of living high at the cost of the poor: the wealthiest fifth of the world's population consumes astonishingly eighty-six percent of all the world's goods and services, while the poorest fifth consumes one percent.

In an atheistic *dog eat dog* world, in secularism's pleasure and preference oriented world where selfishness, self-centeredness, and the avoidance of pain and suffering at all costs is promoted, where the cult of the body is the new practice of worship, the plight of the poor and disenfranchised is irrelevant. Where nominalism, pragmaticism, egoism, hedonism, evolutionism, positivism and relativism reign, as they do in secularism, myths such as these flourish.

The pharmaceutical companies and Planned Parenthood, the world's leading abortion provider, have tremendous profits at stake in promoting the overpopulation myth. Their agenda is quite simple: contraception, abortion, sterilization.

Alan Guttmacher, the former director of the International Planned Parenthood Federation, made that agenda quite clear when he stated: "[Our objective is] compulsory sterilization and compulsory abortion."

Planned Parenthood—which perhaps has the greatest to gain from this myth—is not shy in using deceptive tactics, such as the one they used in a 1985 campaign: *"The human race has 35 years left; after that people will start eating plankton, or people."*[30]

When one worships the secular gods of money, of self-pleasuring, of survival of the fittest, of the beautiful and healthy, then innocents die!

Let us look at the real facts. If you took the entire population of the world, it could fit comfortably into the state of Texas, with a no greater population density than New Jersey. According to the *U.S. Printing Office* the world's population in the year 2001 was 6.15 billion with a growth rate of .02 percent. Since 1900, food production has exceeded population increases. According to the *United Nations' Population Information Network*, the world's population will grow to 7.3 billion by the year 2040 and then level off.

While it is true that the population in so-called *third world* countries is increasing, the population in many so-called *first world* countries is on the decline. In Italy, the birth rate does not equal the death rate, thus failing to even reach the level of replacement. This is not an unusual phenomenon in the richest parts of the world where secularism is the religion of the people. After all, more children, more costs, smaller house, less cars, less entertainment, more work!

The fact that the world's population is in no danger of overpopulating the earth or in over-consuming the world's resources, does not mean that everything is okay. Efforts can be made to better the situation. However, the secular, atheistic quick fix, immoral approach is not only disastrous but ineffective.

Much of the population control being done in the world is not through Natural Family Planning and economic and industrial development, but through the evil means of abortion, sterilization, and contraception. Through abortion, sterilization, and contraception minds are being damaged, morals are being devastated, families are losing their traditional tightly knit structure, and the sense of the sacred and the transcendental is slowly being eroded.

In the name of combating hunger and population control, people who support abortion, contraception and sterilization are people that often misunderstand the poorest of the poor. Couples in the so-called *third world* have large families (i.e., five or more children) not out of ignorance but out of necessity. In the West we have social security and a pension plan when we retire. In the *third world* social security is found not in a check but in a couple's children. Since one out of ten children die before the age of five in these poorest of poor countries, a couple's only means of survival into old age (when they can no longer work the fields, etc.) is to have children to take care of them. The more children one has the greater chance that some will survive to take care of them.

The wealthy countries must be willing to help in the development of the less fortunate nations, and they must be willing to share their excess of resources. As was mentioned before, the wealthiest fifth of the world's population consumes astonishingly eighty-six percent of all the world's goods and services, while the poorest fifth consumes one percent. A more generous heart is needed, even if our standard of living decreases. As Mother Teresa of Calcutta said: "It is a poverty to decide that a child must die so that we may live as we wish."

What then is the answer? When Margaret Sanger, the founder of Planned Parenthood, attempted to introduce contraceptives into India, Mahatma Gandhi reprimanded Sanger by pointing out that what India needed was not contraceptives but "the proper land system, better agriculture and supplementary industry." If this was done, Gandhi continued, "India would be capable of supporting twice as many people."

Pope John Paul II, in his work *Evangelium Vitae*, summed up the Catholic teaching on population management and authentic development:

Governments and various national agencies must above all strive to create economic, social, public health and cultural conditions which will enable married couples to make their choices about procreation in full freedom and with genuine responsibility (i.e., using natural family planning). They must make efforts to ensure greater opportunities and a fairer distribution of wealth so that everyone can share equitably in the goods of creation. Solutions must be sought on the global level by establishing a true economy of communion and sharing of goods, in both the national and international order. This is the only way to respect the dignity of persons and families, as well as the authentic cultural patrimony of peoples.[31]

This is a complete absurdity to the secular view of survival of the fittest and self-pleasuring. As one man said to me quite bluntly, "I won't give a penny to lower my standard of living." When I mentioned that children could die because of his inaction he said, "Let them die!" Only in a mind so absorbed in the self can such thoughts exists. Only in the mind of an atheist!

God exists because the world disintegrates when it represses his existence. God exists because the world is "wired" for him!

HUMAN CLONING—ATHEISM GONE WILD[32]

We are going to be one with God. We are going to have almost as much knowledge and almost as much power as God.
   Richard Sheed,
   National Public Radio, 1998

In theory, human cloning is a way of producing a genetic replica of a person without sexual reproduction.

Cloning occurs when the nuclear material from a cell of an organism's body (a somatic cell) is transplanted into a female reproductive cell (an oocyte) whose nuclear material has been removed or inactivated in order to produce a new, genetically identical organism.

Those who favor cloning argue that one could theoretically harvest cells, blood, tissues, and much needed organs such as hearts, livers and kidneys for therapeutic use.

These harvested *products* would be considered ideal for they would be immunologically matched—that is, they would eliminate the need for life-long immunosuppressive therapy.

At another level, cloning would provide a means for sterile couples to reproduce.

At a glance cloning may appear appealing to some but in reality it is radically evil. As the ethicist Hans Jonas has written, "[Human cloning] is the most despotic . . . and the most slavish form of genetic manipulation."[33]

The *Pontificia Academia Pro Vita* in its "Reflections on Cloning" points out that human cloning would radically damage the meaning, rationality, and complimentarity of human reproduction:

- The unitive, bonding aspect of human sexual reproduction would be lost in cloning. The precious gift of sexual intercourse as a physical and spiritual act between a man and a woman would become non-existent. A woman in theory could take the nuclear material from a somatic cell from her body and fuse it into her own ovum and produce a genetic reproduction of herself without any need of a husband.

- The naturally occurring balance between the male and female sex in society as well as the natural structure of the family would inevitably become distorted. As the document "Reflections on Cloning" explains: It is conceivable that "a woman could [end up being] the twin sister of her mother, lack a biological father and be the daughter of her grandfather."

- Human life would become viewed more as a *product*, an object to be harvested, rather than as a gift of love. Cloning would suppress personal identity and subjectivity at the cost of biological qualities that could be appraised and selected. Women would be exploited for their ova and their wombs, being seen simply in terms of their *purely biological functions*.

- Cloning could lead to a loss of genetic variation in society, thereby making society vulnerable to catastrophic illnesses and genetic defects. Naturally occurring mutations would not be sufficient to assure genetic variation.

- Cloning would lead to a wide array of psychological problems, whereby one would be troubled by questions such as: Who is my father? Who is my mother? Do I even have a father and mother? Who am I? What am I? Where do I come from?

- Cloning could lead to even greater trauma in the lives of parents who have lost a beloved child. The assumption from some heartbroken parents would be that if they could only clone their dead child, they would somehow have him or her back again. But this is not the case. A cloned individual would have a different guiding life principle and a different cultural and environmental upbringing. This child would not be what they desired or intended. Abuse of that cloned child could soon follow.

- One's *quality of life* would become a surrogate for one's search for meaning and salvation. A culture that is already self-centered and selfish would become even more so. It would become an even more *I, me, mine culture*, even more an atheistic culture.

- Human cloning could be the ultimate expression of narcissism and hedonism. One could envision a world that desires to clone only the so-called *beautiful* people. And who determines who are the beautiful people? Furthermore, one could envision a society in which a self-absorbed person would clone himself or herself so as to have spare parts in the event of illnesses.

- And finally, but most importantly, cloning would assault the dignity of human life in the most cruel and exploitative way imaginable by making cloned children the subject of experiments and by preventing their births.

- Dr. Ian Wilmut was only capable of producing Dolly, the cloned sheep, after 277 attempts at cloning. In terms of human beings no culture could morally sustain itself by killing 277 human embryos with the hope of one surviving, nor allow for the current rate of 95 to 99 percent of embryos to die in the process of cloning.

Richard Sheed's words echo ominously: "We are going to become one with God. We are going to have almost as much knowledge and almost as much power as God." Cloning is an experiment in playing God. Atheists like playing and being God!

God exists because the world disintegrates when it represses his existence. God exists because the world is "wired" for him!

EMBRYONIC STEM CELL RESEARCH[34]

Stem cells are cells that have not undergone maturation and theoretically can become any of the 220 cell types and any of the 210 specialized tissue types that make up the human body.

Because stem cells are like *blank slates*, they theoretically can morph into any kind of human tissue. They theoretically can become replacement parts for unhealthy cells and tissues. The benefits from stem cell research provides the future with great possibilities in the cure and treatment of illnesses, such as Parkinson's, Alzheimer's, heart disease, and diabetes.

Stem cells can be obtained immorally by the destruction of human life (i.e., human embryos) or they can be obtained morally from adults in a safe manner (i.e., from muscles, umbilical cords, bone marrow, the placenta, and from a wide variety of other adult tissues). Atheism has embraced embryonic stem cell research with a passion.

The reality is that embryonic stem cells have never helped a human patient.[35]

During the National Academy of Sciences' workshop in 2001 on "Stem Cells and the Future of Regenerative Medicine" held in Washington, D.C., Marcus Grompe, M.D., Ph.D., an expert in molecular and medical genetics, stated: "There is no evidence of therapeutic benefit from embryonic stem cells," and Dr. Bert Vogelstein, chairman of John Hopkins University's Institute of Medicine studying stem cell research pointed out that any therapeutic claim of benefit from embryonic stem cell research is purely "conjectural."[36]

On the other hand, great success has been attained in the use of adult stem cells. Adult stem cells not only have a future in curing and treating illnesses, they are doing so right now. Adult stem cells are currently being used in the treatment of multiple sclerosis, lupus, rheumatoid arthritis, stroke, anemia, Epstein-Barr virus infection, cornea damage, blood and liver diseases, brain tumors, retinoblastoma, ovarian cancer, solid tumors, testicular cancer, leukemia, breast cancer, neuroblastoma, non-Hodgkins' lymphoma, renal cell carcinoma, diabetes, heart damage, as well as cartilage, bone, muscle, and spinal-cord damage.[37]

Given the benefits of adult stem cells, the question must be asked: Why are so many individuals preoccupied with embryonic stem cell research which involves the destruction of human life? Given the success of adult stem cells, you would think that these individuals would want improved funding and research in the field of adult stem cell experimentation.[38]

The preoccupation with embryonic stem cells is an assault on the dignity of human life and a hindrance to the advancement of sound, moral science. It is a perfect expression of "let others die so that I can live as I wish!" It is the ultimate in egoistic secularism which worships self-preservation and the avoidance of discomfort, suffering, or pain at all costs! It is the ultimate in the *pleasure principle* gone wild. It is the ultimate in pragmaticism, of using up others and then throwing them away when they are no longer of value. It is the ultimate in positivism where emotional and psychological attitudes override logic!

Recent advances in adult stem cell research have made embryonic stem cell research unnecessary. Why does this research persist, then? If one accepts human life at it earliest stages, in its embryonic form, then you will have to accept it at later stages! *The abortion and contraceptive industries have much at stake in this battle!*

Denying life at its earliest stages opens the door to denying life at its latter stages. Death begets death!

God exists because the world disintegrates when it represses his existence. God exists because the world is "wired" for him!

GENETIC ENGINEERING, ASSISTED REPRODUCTION, SCIENTIFIC RESEARCH

Scientific research that aims at eliminating or overcoming sterility is of great merit as long as it seeks to maintain the unitive and procreative dimensions of the sexual act. It is gravely immoral to separate a husband from his wife (and vice versa) by introducing a third person into the reproductive process.

But that is exactly what atheism promotes in the name of self-interest, self-centeredness, self-pleasuring, and emotional comfort. In the name of secularism society is harmed because the very nature or essence of the family—which secularism implicitly denies—is disastrously manipulated and quite often destroyed. Children become possessions—no more than a family dog, and sometimes less valued than the family dog.

In the Catholic document *Donum Vitae* II, 1, 5, 4 we read:[39]

Techniques that entail the disassociation of husband and wife, by the intrusion of a person other than the couple (donation of sperm, or ovum, surrogate uterus), are gravely immoral. These techniques (heterologous artificial insemination and fertilization) infringe the child's right to be born of a father and mother known to him and bound to each other by marriage. They betray the spouses' right to become a father and a mother only through each other.

Techniques involving only the married couple (homologous artificial insemination and fertilization) are perhaps less reprehensible, yet remain morally unacceptable. They dissociate the sexual act from the procreative act. The act which brings the child into existence is no longer an act by which two persons give themselves to one another, but one that 'entrusts the life and identity of the embryo into the power of doctors and biologists and establishes the domination of technology over the origin and destiny of the human person. Such a relationship of domination is in itself contrary to the dignity and equality that must be common to parents and children.' Under the moral aspect procreation is deprived of its proper perfection when it is not willed as the fruit of the conjugal act, that is to say, of the specific act of the spouses' union . . . Only respect for the link between the meanings of the conjugal act and respect for the unity of the human being make possible procreation in conformity with the dignity of the person.

At the heart of sexuality is the inseparable bond between the unitive and procreative dimensions of the conjugal act. This reality can be a tremendous cross upon a couple that so much desires the gift of a child.

It must be remembered that children are not property owed to a couple. No one has a *right to a child*. Only the child has rights, *the right to be the fruit of the specific act of the conjugal love of his parents*, and *the right to be respected as a person from the moment of conception*.

Those who are unable to have children by moral means should be encouraged to become generative by their works of charity and to seek the alternative of adoption, the giving of a loving home for parentless children, children hungering for the love of parents.

Atheism wants nothing to do with this! Abortion not adoption, my child, not my gift, my possession, my desires, my fulfillment, my preference, my pleasure, my genes, my immortality through my child, my, my, my, my. . . .

(A child that grows up without the love of a parent is predisposed to the personality disorder of atheism.)

God exists because the world disintegrates when it represses his existence. God exists because the world is "wired" for him!

DESIGNER BABIES

When one is able to clone or to select what sex, hair or eye color, intellect, body structure, and so forth by genetic engineering and the manipulation and choice of embryos, one is going down a dangerous path. Huge distortions in the gene pool—which is essential for a healthy population—and huge distortions in the balance of the sexes in the population are bound to occur— cultures that prefer male children (often poor countries) will be overpopulated with males and cultures that favor female children will be overpopulated with females. Designer babies will lead to distorted populations susceptible to grave illnesses, because of the diminished gene pool and the imbalance of the sexes.

The striking, unique and unrepeatable qualities that make each of us special and distinctively beautiful are at stake when a culture seeks to play God. A culture that flirts with manipulating the origins of life is a culture flirting with extinction.

Atheism gone wild: my desires, my right, my fulfillment, my preference, my pleasure, my creation, my body, my, my, my, my....

An Often Overlooked Reality of Cloning, Embryonic Stem Cell Research, and Invitro-Fertilization

One of the often overlooked evils associated with the above practices is that in the process of cloning, or doing embryonic stem cell research, or attempting to have a child by means of artificial insemination, embryos are exploited and killed during the process. Human beings become biological debris.[40]

HYBRIDIZATION[41]

Hybridization is the combining of two species artificially or naturally so as to form a new species. Hybridization is common in agriculture and even in animals. For example, the hybrid of a horse and a donkey is a mule. The hybrid of a lion and a tiger is called a liger.

In a culture without limits, where God is the self, where atheism is on the rise, it is just a matter of time before scientists attempt to hybridize higher forms of life.

It is quite possible that the future will be inhabited with hybridized humanoids—half human, half something else! The making of all forms of distorted human-like species will wreak havoc on our culture and lead to its genetic disintegration.

This may seem far-fetched, but it is just around the corner! A world infected with atheistic notions is a world capable of anything!

God exists because the world disintegrates when it represses his existence. God exists because the world is "wired" for him!

EUTHANASIA VS. PALLIATIVE CARE—THE END RESULT[42]

I have had lots of patients who wanted to commit suicide, but you don't help them do it. You learn why patients don't want to live anymore. If they're in pain, you give them more or better medication. If they have trouble with their families, you help them get the problem solved.[43]

                                                      Elisabeth Kubler-Ross

Elisabeth Kubler-Ross was a world-renowned medical doctor and psychiatrist. She did much research and wrote several books and articles in the area of death and dying. In her research, she found that people who face death often experience episodes of denial, anger, bargaining, and depression. Most importantly, she pointed out that if a patient was lovingly cared for, the patient's last moments would be ones filled with acceptance and even hope.

Direct euthanasia consists in the murdering of the handicapped, the ill, and the dying—with or without their consent and knowledge. Euthanasia is understood as an action or omission of an action which of itself or by intention causes death in order that all suffering may be eliminated.

Today, too many terminally ill patients are being euthanized before they have come to a stage of acceptance and peace. Too many people are being put to death in times of anger, loneliness, and depression. A great injustice is being done to such people, all in the name of compassion. Those who claim that by eliminating pain, they are being compassionate toward the person, fail to recognize the advances in palliative care.

Palliative care is what should be promoted, not euthanasia. Palliative care is a form of care which seeks to eliminate pain and understands the redemptive value of unavoidable suffering. It encourages the use of painkillers in alleviating suffering. It makes sure that at no stage of a person's illness is the ordinary care owed to a sick person to be interrupted. Anyone who has seen the work of hospice knows how painless and beautiful death can be. It can truly be seen not as an end, but as a natural process of life.

My uncle died at the young age of fifty-eight from terminal cancer. He received the best of palliative care. He died a peaceful, joyous and holy death in the arms of his loving family. Let no one deprive us of this!

In the secular nation of the Netherlands, one out of four people are euthanized, often without their approval. A trip to the hospital is a terrifying experience, especially for the elderly! Don't close your eyes in the Netherlands, you may never open them again!

Atheism has no place for a life that seems no longer useful or is seen as burdensome to others. When the concepts of a person's innate dignity and essence are thrown away, the person is easily thrown away. When life is without pleasure, it is to be euthanized. When one is no longer fit to survive, then one is to be selected out of the population gene pool. *If you are not of value to me or are a hindrance to me, then you are no longer wanted.* Through secularism's dummying down of society, palliative care is ignored or not even recognized, and euthanasia is seen as the only compassionate way to alleviate pain. As the *god of atheism*, Nietzsche, would say, "The thought of suicide is a powerful comfort: it helps one through many a dreadful night."[44] How sad!

God exists because the world disintegrates when it represses his existence. God exists because the world is "wired" for him!

PREMARITAL SEX[45]

It is quite popular in today's secular culture to accept the popular message by educators, healthcare professionals, politicians, entertainers, and those in the media that premarital sex is harmless. The denial of essences, of the natural law, of the unitive and bonding nature of sex, of the nature of woman and man, and of absolutes has denigrated sex to its most base instincts. Is it any wonder that fifty percent of students that graduate from high school will have had premarital sex? Is it any wonder that seventeen percent of children in the seventh or eighth grade report having had sex? One in nine become pregnant![46]

Premarital sex has given rise to an epidemic of sexually transmitted diseases, an epidemic number of abortions, and the ever increasing rise in divorce rates. One point three million new cases of gonorrhea occur every year, with some strains being resistant to penicillin. According to the *Center for Disease Control* sixty-five million Americans are plagued with an incurable form of a sexually transmitted disease.[47] It is estimated that every year some 60,000 to 100,000 young women are made sterile by HIV, gonorrhea or chlamydia. As many as a third of sexually active teenagers have genital warts.

Sexually transmitted diseases infect approximately twelve million Americans each year. Two-thirds of sexually transmitted diseases occur in persons younger than twenty-five and every year more than three million teenagers are infected. This epidemic has caused many women to have problems with infertility—STD's being the fastest growing cause of infertility.[48] It is estimated that one out of four adults have an STD.[49]

The epidemic in infections caused by premarital sex has led to the secular mirage of *safe sex*. The CDC refers to safe sex as oral sex, mutual masturbation, and sex with a condom—and if *safe sex* fails then abortion or the morning after pill, the morning after abortion is waiting. Each year 400,000 young women under twenty will have an abortion, and within a year after their pregnancy, one in five will become pregnant again and seek another abortion. Nearly one-half of all pregnancies are unintended.[50]

Premarital sex increases the divorce rate. Men have an innate desire to marry a virgin. Men who know that their wives have had a long sex life prior to marriage have a tendency of viewing their wives, whether consciously or unconsciously, as impure or even loose.

Statistics point to people engaged in premarital sex as having an increase in emotional and psychological problems, an increase in marital difficulties, and a proneness to engage in high-risk behavior detrimental to family and marital life.[51]

This atheistic mentality regarding premarital sex has led to a separation of sex from its unitive and bonding nature. It has separated it from its transcendental and spiritual aspects. It has debased it to the level of an animal instinct—which is contrary to its innate, natural order of being. But if there are no such things as innate realities according to the natural order of things, and if there are no essences to things and actions, then all is a matter of evolutionistic compulsion and slavery to the appetites.

Popular secularism has deified premarital sex, and it has therefore contaminated society with an infection it may never be able to cure.

God exists because the world disintegrates when it represses his existence. God exists because the world is "wired" for him!

DIVORCE—IMPACTING THE FUTURE[52]

Children of two parent families are statistically healthier, physically and mentally, than children of divorced parents or children from single parent homes. They do better in terms of mental health, happiness, life expectancy, and career success. They are more likely to have a happy marriage and a happy family.[53]

Even children who live in an unhappy marriage do better than children who live in a divorced arrangement. Statistics point out that even argumentative parents tend to have happier and healthier children than divorced parents.[54]

Children of divorced parents get less education, are less successful in adulthood, are more prone to drugs, premarital sex, illicit pregnancy, and getting divorced themselves when they marry. Children of divorce parents tend to be more reckless and prone to accidents. The scars of divorce tend to follow them through life and have a tendency of shortening their life expectancy. Divorce also increases the likelihood of a child growing up to be an atheist. [55]

Remarriage does not improve things for children; in fact, in some cases it worsens the situation. Children who live in homes where a second marriage has taken place are dozens of times more likely to be the victims of violence and sexual abuse and they tend to live a far less healthy, happy, and stable life.[56]

To make things worse, seventy percent of second marriages, eighty-seven percent of third marriages, and ninety-three percent of fourth marriages break up within five years.[57]

Young boys are particularly affected by divorce. Seeing their mother with another man can leave traumatic scars. Often these children grow up resenting women as being *cheap* or promiscuous. This not only devastates relationships but society in general.

A poor parental image in the mind of a child is one of the major factors, if that role model is not substituted for by another, for atheism.

God exists because the world disintegrates when it represses his existence. God exists because the world is "wired" for him!

VIOLENCE IN SOCIETY—THE BEGINNINGS OF THE END

With adjustments to population growth, the *FBI Uniform Crime Report* confirms that four decades of secularism, four decades of pragmaticism, nominalism, egoism, ultiltarianism, hedonism, evolutionism, positivism, relativism, and four decades of the philosophy of the survival of the fittest has brought our society to the edge of collapse.

In 1960 there were 3,095,700 incidents of property crime, 9,110 incidents of murder, 17,190 incidents of rape, 107,840 incidents of robbery, 154,320 incidents of aggravated assault, 912,100 incidents of burglary, and 328,200 incidents of vehicle theft.

What has happened in the four decades where the religion of secularism has flourished? In the year 2007 there were 9,843,481 incidents of property crime, 16,929 incidents of murder, 90,427 incidents of rape, 445,125 incidents of robbery, 910,744 incidents of aggravated assault, 2,179,140 incidents of burglary, and 1,095,769 incidents of car theft.[58]

This is the great utopia that the religion of secular humanism, of atheism, has brought us! As atheistic philosophies permeate the minds and hearts of more and more people, a resorting to the survival of the fittest, a resorting to *man's* most base instincts is likely to occur.

What is said statistically of the United States is simply a reflection of all secular societies that have sought to secularize their countries.

IN CONCLUSION

We were meant for God. We were "wired" for God. Denying this reality leads to the fracturing of societies. The fact that atheism leads to the disintegration of societies is a *convincing and converging* proof for the existence of God.

It is quite obvious that the religion of atheism, the religion of *chance*, of *deficient science*, of Darwinism is a barbaric one. Genocide, infanticide, ethnic cleansing, callous racism, and an unforgiving, petty, unjust, vindictive, bloodthirsty world are the result of such a worldview!

After reading the above, can anyone doubt the existence of an atheist personality disorder? Can anyone doubt a blindness to the consequences of atheism held by atheists?

NOTES

1. Charles Darwin, *The Descent of Man* (Princeton: Princeton University Press, 1981), pt. I, ch. III, 76–77. This is why a morality without a God is a morality of survival of the fittest, which is nothing other than anarchy lived out. Even Richard Dawkins' *The God Delusion* recognizes a purely Darwinian approach to morality as inadequate, 219–222; In *The Selfish Gene*, 2–3, he explains, "Be warned that if you wish, as I do, to build a society in which individuals cooperate generously and unselfishly towards the common good, you can expect little help from biological nature. Let us try to teach generosity and altruism, because we are born selfish." Ludwig Feuerbach likewise recognized in his Essence of Christianity that "survival of the fittest" could not be a moral code.

2. Dennett, *Darwin's Dangerous Idea*, 500.

3. Quoted in Paul C. Vitz, *The Faith of the Fatherless: The Psychology of Atheism* (Dallas: Spence Publishing, Co., 1999), 137.

4. Zbigniew Brzezinski, *Out of Control*, (New York: Touchstone, 1995), 17.

5. Detailed analysis of "when human life begins" can be found in Benedict Ashley, *Health Care Ethics*, 4th ed., (Washington: Georgetown University Press, 1997), 227–235.

6. *NCCB, Life-Insights*, March-April, 2001.

7. Pasquini, *Pro-Life* (New York: iUniverse, 2003), 5–8.

8. *Evangelium Vitae*, n. 13. *Health Care Ethics*, 271–307. Contraception and Natural Family Planning are discussed in CCC 2370 and 2399.

9. *Health Care Ethics*, 252–263; CCC 2270–2272, 2274.

10. Atheists such as Richard Dawkins have accused God as being the biggest abortionist because of miscarriages. Dawkins fails to recognize the concept of original sin and its distortion upon creation. Dawkins is also playing loose with the facts. The fact is that one out of four children conceived in the United States, alone, is aborted, one every twenty-two seconds! This does not take into account the unknown number of abortions that occur from contraceptives! Furthermore, evidence shows that syngamy, when not successfully complete, leads to miscarriages. In many cases the ova has been penetrated by the sperm, but not efficiently enough to be called syngamy—a miscarriage usually follows. Cf. *Health Care Ethics*, 235–236; James Diamond, "Abortion, Animation, and Biological Hominization," *Theological Studies* 36, 1975, 305–324; Allen Wilcox, "Incidence of Early Loss of Pregnancy," *New England Journal of Medicine* 319 (4), July 28, 1988, 189–194. One final point, the Church has never taught the existence of Limbo as an official teaching. Children that die through miscarriages go to heaven by virtue of a baptism of desire, the desire of all the faithful. The early Church always recognized three forms of baptism: baptism by desire, by blood, and by water. You should know the belief system of your opponents before making misleading assertions. Are we not all looking for truth?

11. Clowes, *Facts of Life*, 15.

12. John Pasquini, *Pro-Life* (New York: iUniverse, 2003), 17–21; Also, Cf. Theresa Burke, *Forbidden Grief* (Springfield: Acorn Books, 2002); Jeanette Vought, *Post Abortion Trauma* (Grand Rapids: Zondervan, 1991); Pam Koerbel, *Abortions Second Victim* (Wheaton: Victor Books, 1986); David Reardon, *Aborted Women—Silent No More* (Westchester: Crossway Books, 1987); Teri and Paul Reiser, *Help for Post-Abortion Woman* (Grand Rapids: Zondervan, 1989).

13. For a comprehensive theology/philosophy of sex see Vincent Genovesi, *In Pursuit of Love*, 2nd ed. (Collegeville: The Liturgical Press, 1996); K.D. Whitehead, "Sex Education: Vatican Guidelines." *Crisis*, vol. 13, n. 5 (May 1996).

14. A.S. Antonisamy, *Wisdom for All Times: Mahatma Gandhi and Pope Paul VI on Birth Regulation* (Pondicherry: Family Life Service Center, 1978).

15. *The Truth and Meaning of Human Sexuality*, Vatican City, 1995, paragraphs 3, 4, 16, 17, 18, 22, 65–76.

16. Ibid., 4.

17. Ibid., 14.

18. Clowes, *Facts of Life*, 276–277.

19. Cf. *In Pursuit of Love*, 127–129; CCC 2211, 2354, 2396.

20. Sanger, *The Woman Rebel*, vol. 1, n. 1, reprinted in *Woman in the New Race* (New York: Brentanos Publishers, 1922).

21. Cf. *Family Safe Media* (January 10, 2006); *National Research Council Report*, 3–1, 2002; *Family Safe Media* (December 15, 2005); www.freedomyou.com/ addiction/ Internet_Pornography.htm.; About.com:Sexuality (October 2, 2008).

22. *Truth and Meaning of Human Sexuality: Pontifical Council for the Family: Vatican City* (December 8, 1995).

23. *Philadelphia Inquirer*, Jan. 9, 1987.

24. These statistics were compiled by the *National Institute on Drug Abuse Report and Child Abuse and Neglect Study* by Arthur Becker-Weidman: www.childhelp .org/resources/learning-center/statistics.; CDC publication: www.cdc.gov/mmwr.; www.childabuse.com/fs0.htm.; *National Clearinghouse on Child Abuse and Neglect: Long-term consequences of Child Abuse and Neglect*, 2005; *National Institute on Drug Abuse 2000 Report.*

25. Causes, solutions, and obligations toward the poor, CCC 194, 517, 525, 544, 786, 852, 866, 1033, 1351, 1397, 1435, 1825, 2204–2206, 2407, 2439–2440, 2443–2449.

26. CCC 2448; *Libertatis conscientia*, 68.

27. *Briefing Paper, Hunger on the Rise: Food and Agriculture Organization* (September 17, 2008); *Are We On Track To End Hunger Report 2004: Bread for the World Institute*, 2004; *State of Food Insecurity in the World 2002: Food and Agriculture Organization of the United Nations*; *State of the World's Children 2008—Child Survival: UNICEF*, January 2008; Robert Black and Jennifer Bryce: *Where and Why are 10 Million Children Dying Every Year? The Lancet* 361: 2226–2234 (2003); Low Birth weight: *World Health Organization*, 2004.

28. *Hom. In Lazaro*, 2,5: PG 48, 992.

29. acqueline Kasun, *War Against Population* (San Francisco: Ignatius Press, 1999).

30. Cf. Clowes, *Facts of Life*, 299–328.

31. *Evangelium Vitae*, n. 91.

32. Cf. *Dignitas Personae*, 28–30.

33. Hans Jonas, *Tecnica, medicina edetica*, 1997.

34. The holy and unholy use of stem cells, *Dignitas Personae*, 31–32.

35. *NCCB, Life Issue Forum*, 2001; *Science*, April, 2001.

36. *NCCB, Life Issue Forum*, 2001; Science, April, 2001; *Lancet*, January 2001; APR, 2000.

37. Ibid.

38. The anthropological, theological and ethical aspects of human life and procreation are addressed in *Dignitas Personae*, 4–23.

39. *Donum Vitae II*, 1, 5, 4. CCC 2274–2275, 2288–2296; *Dignitas Personae*, 12–13, 25–27.

40. *Dignitas Personae*, 12–13, 25–27.

41. Hybridization is addressed in *Dignitas Personae*, 33.

42. CCC 2276–2279.

43. Cf. Elisabeth Kubler-Ross, *Death and Dying* (New York: MacmIlllan, 1993), 75, 75–98.

44. *Basic Writings of Nietzsche*, 281.

45. Overview of key principles found in Genovesi, *In Pursuit of Love*, 147–181; CCC 1755, 1852, 2353.

46. Cf. *The Surgeon General's Call to Action to Promote Sexual Health*, 2001.

47. CDC, 2005.

48. *The Surgeon General's Call to Action to Promote Sexual Health*, 2001.

49. *Center for Disease Control and Prevention*, November 2007.

50. Ibid.

51. CDC, 2005.

52. CCC 1650, 1651, 1664, 2382–2386, 2400.

53. Cf. Waite and Gallagher, *The Case for Marriage*.

54. *Journal of Adolescent Research* 1, 1986: 389–97.

55. *The Case for Marriage*, 129–140.

56. *Child Abuse and Neglect* 8, 1984: 15–22; *Journal of the American Academy of Child and Adolescent Psychiatry* 20, no. 3, May 1991:358–9.

57. *All About Families*, April 26, 2000, 1–2.

58. *FBI Uniform Crime Report: US Department of Justice*, 2007.

XV

Concluding Remarks

ATHEISM'S ASSUMPTION

Atheists assume—whether consciously or not--that the mind is capable or will be capable of knowing all things! What is the reason behind such an assertion? What makes the atheist think that his or her brain is capable of all knowledge? What makes a human brain all-knowing, and that of a monkey limited? When compared to God, our capacity for knowledge is as great as that of a cockroach—and I am overestimating the cockroach's ability.

If one accepts that the human mind will always be limited, then how can one be so certain of God's non-existence! I have *Pascal's Wager* to hang my hat on, but the atheist has only delusions of omnipotence!

CONVERGING ARGUMENTS

The above arguments are not meant to prove the existence of God in the same way that science proves a hypothesis. They are not proofs in the manner of the *natural sciences*. Rather, the *proofs* here must be seen as *converging and convincing arguments* that call one to question the plausibility for the existence of God. And when one studies the plausibility of the arguments one is left with the reality that the probability for God's existence is much more likely than his non-existence!

Atheism collapses if the theory of evolution collapses. For the Catholic, whether God created in an instance or through a process of evolution has no impact on Catholic theology. When we take the cumulative weight of the arguments favoring the existence of God, the evidence is overwhelming.

Appendix I

Psychology of Atheism:[1]
The Atheist Personality Disorder

There are essentially three types of atheists. One form of atheism is referred to as *categorical atheism*; this form of atheism is based on a reasoned, reflected inability to comprehend the possibility for the existence of God. It becomes *militant atheism* when this type of atheism is attached to a desire for converting God-believers. *Practical atheism* is a worldview where the question of God's existence is irrelevant to the meaning of life and the decisions of human existence: The belief or disbelief in God is irrelevant, for life, for such people, is lived out in a way that is indistinguishable from that of the categorical atheist.

It is quite clear from the interviews and writings of famous categorical, militant, and practical atheists that atheism is a disorder. Atheism is a personality disorder, and for some, an un-repairable psychopathic disorder.

Treatment of the *atheist personality disorder* requires the uncovering of the conscious and subconscious wounds and traumas that predispose a person to atheism. With counseling, and medication, atheism can be managed and even healed.

The following theories have been proposed by many, in one form or another, as having a causal relationship to the development of atheism. The following will make it quite apparent that the preventing of atheism is easier than the curing of it. Fostering healthy families is the most effective means for preventing the *atheist personality disorder*.

THE DEFECTIVE FATHER

Paul C. Vitz has proposed the *theory of the defective father* to explain atheism. The representation of God as a *father figure* is well documented in the

97

scientific literature. Psychologists, psychoanalysts, anthropologists, and sociologist have confirmed this connection over the years.[2] As Freud explained: "Psychoanalysis daily demonstrates to us how youthful persons lose their religious faith as soon as the authority of the father breaks down."[3]

God has traditionally been seen, implicitly or explicitly, as an authority figure, a father figure. The *theory of the defective father* argues that those who have had absent fathers (due to early death, abandonment or aloofness), or who have had weak fathers (cowardly or fearful) or abusive fathers (psychologically or sexually), have trouble recognizing God. It is hard to pray "Our Father, who art in heaven" when one's *father-image* is defective. (*The exception would be for those who have found adequate substitutes for the absent, weak or abusive father.*)

The following is a list of the world's most famous categorical, militant and practical atheists and how they fit in with the theory of the defective father:

Nietzsche's father died before he was five. Reflecting upon the death of his father he wrote: "Transfixed by the idea of being separated for ever from my beloved father, I wept bitterly. . . . I will never forget the gloomy melody of the hymn 'Jesus my faith.'"[4] Six months later, his younger brother died.

David Hume's father, Joseph, died when he was two years old, leaving him with a sense of bitterness and anger.

Bertrand Russell's father, Lord Amberly, died when Bertrand was four. His mother died two years earlier. His grandfather, a possible father substitute, died when he was six. A nanny whom he became attached to abandoned the family when he was eleven.

Jean Paul Sartre's father, Jean Baptiste, died when Sartre was fifteen months old. His mother would abandon Sartre upon remarriage. Jean Paul was left with his grandparents. Sartre viewed his grandparents as old, weak, and manipulative.

Albert Camus' father, Lucien, died when Albert was one. No father substitutes could be found for Camus.

Arthur Schopenhauer's father, Floris, committed suicide when Arthur was seventeen. Without any maternal love, and a deep sense that his mother was to blame for his father's death, Arthur would suffer a lifelong fear of abandonment.

Thomas Hobbes, while more a deist[5] than an atheist, was clearly anti-Church and anti-clerical. His father, whose name was also Thomas, left home at an early age and died in obscurity. Hobbes was a practical as opposed to categorical atheist.

Jean Meslier, although a priest, was an atheist. As he would say of himself, "I was never a believer." Jean was forced into the priesthood and into a celibate life by his father. After Meslier's death, his atheism came to light through his anti-clerical, pro and pre-revolution writings.

Voltaire, a deist or practical atheist, was anti-Church and anti-clerical. When seven years old his mother died, and his father sent him away for schooling. Suspecting that he was an illegitimate child, he changed his name from Arouet to Voltaire, thereby disavowing his family heritage.

Jean d'Alembert was born out of an illegitimate relationship and abandoned in a wicker basket in front of a Catholic Church.

Ludwig Feuerbach viewed his father as impulsive and volatile. His father Anselm abandoned him and his mother when he was nine. Anselm moved in with his mistress Nannette Brunner. He would only return to his wife and son upon the death of his mistress.

Samuel Butler was often beaten by his father in childhood. In adulthood father and son publicly expressed their mutual hate for each other.

Sigmund Freud referred to his father as a sexual pervert and as a weak man—passive in his response to anti-Semitism.

Joseph Stalin and his mother received severe beatings from Joseph's alcoholic father.

Mao Zedong viewed his father as a tyrant.

Karl Marx's viewed his father as bourgeois and saw him as a weak man who converted to Christianity for superficial reasons, for social and political advancement.

While Adolf Hitler was a pagan more than an atheist his anti-Catholicism, anti-Semitism, and anti-Protestantism was highly influenced by the atheist icons Schopenhauer and Nietzsche.[6]

Richard Carlyle's father was an alcoholic and died when Richard was four. No substitute father figure could be found.

Madalyn Murray O'Hair, who is responsible for the banning of prayer in public schools, hated her father with a passion. She once took a knife and threatened to kill him. In her words, "I'll see you dead. I'll get you yet. I'll walk on your grave."[7]

Kate Millet was abandoned by her father at the age of thirteen. Her father ran off with a nineteen year old girl. Kate would express her disappointment by declaring that she would never allow a man to become important in her life.[8]

Daniel Dennett, one of the *new atheists*, lost his father in a plane crash when he was five. His predilection for controversial, antagonistic topics and positions is also indicative or expressive of an inner, unhealed wound. His low self-esteem is expressed in his need for incessantly identifying himself as an atheist.

Mary Ann Cotton, a practical atheist, had a weak father figure who died in a mining accident when Mary was eight. Mary's mother remarried. Her stepfather was stern and inflicted Mary with severe punishments. Mary would kill four husbands, a lover, and several children.

Women who have had defective fathers often grow up to hate men. They often become atheistic feminists.

Defective fathers foster atheism.

THE DEFECTIVE MOTHER

The figure of *mother* is often depicted as God's purity, wisdom, and tenderness in the Hebrew Scriptures and in many world religions. Many of the above atheists also had defective mothers.

The *theory of the defective mother* argues that those who have had poor mother figures (especially promiscuous mothers) or abusive mothers (psychologically or sexually) have trouble recognizing God.

Arthur Schopenhauer's mother was distant and uncaring. Schopenhauer was the product of an unwanted pregnancy. Schopenhauer blamed his mother for his father's suicide.

Albert Ellis's mother was distant and unaffectionate. While hospitalized for nearly a year as a result of a childhood illness, his mother rarely visited him.

Jill Johnston was deceived by her mother and abandoned by her father. It was later found that Jill's parents were never married. Jill's mother would call her daughter a "bastard" and in turn she would call her mother a "whore."[9]

Bertrand Russell lost his mother at the tender age of two.

Jean Paul Sartre's mother, after the death of her first husband, remarried a man who openly rejected Jean Paul. Sartre's mother, after the remarriage, became distant and abandoned him to his aloof grandparents.

Voltaire's mother was an absent figure and was viewed by Voltaire as promiscuous.

John Toland viewed his mother as immoral.

Jean d"Alembert and Baron d'Holbach had absent mother figures.

A defective mother fosters atheism.

THEORY OF THE ABSENT TRINITY

We often, as Christians, use the analogy that the love between the Father and Son is the Holy Spirit. The Trinity is a communion of *Persons* and therefore is relational by nature. Being that we are created in the image of the Trinity, and being that our family is created in the image of the Trinity, it follows that our relationship to God is impacted by how well our family and the family in general models the Trinity.

H.G. Wells' parents were cold to each other, and slept in separate rooms. After the death of Wells' sister, the parents, Joseph and Sarah, lost their faith. H.G. Wells' parents despised each other.

Albert Ellis' crude, vulgar and virulent hatred for religion finds its origins in his relationship with his parents. His mother was distant and unaffectionate, and his father was seldom around and abandoned the family when Albert was in his teens. At five, when Ellis was hospitalized with a serious illness, his family rarely visited him.[10]

Bertrand Russell's mother died when he was two and his father died when he was four. His grandfather died when he was six, and his grandmother had an unappealing temperament. The only substitute for love was a nanny, and she would abandon him when he was eleven years old.

Voltaire's mother died when he was seven. His father was distant. Voltaire believed that he was the illegitimate child of the poet Rochebrune.

Jean d'Alembert was the illegitimate son of a salon hostess and an artillery officer. He was abandoned in a wicker basket in front of a local Church. His father died when Jean was twelve.

Baron d'Holbach was abandoned by his parents and raised by his uncle, whom he had no particular affection for.

Ludwig Feuerbach's father was volatile and unfaithful to his wife. His father would abandon the family to live with a mistress, Nannette Brunner.

If the love within a family does not model the image of the love within the Trinity, then one's intellectual predilections are likely to be affected. Divorce—as earlier sections have pointed out—has had a tremendous impact on the growth of atheism. The prison system is filled with persons who come from damaged families.

If the love within the family does not model the image of the love of God, then a person is likely to become an atheist and also likely to have trouble forming a healthy family: *Atheists are less likely to marry, more likely to divorce, and more likely to have few children.*

POST-ABORTION TRAUMA SYNDROME— A FAMILY TRAUMA

Women who have had an abortion often experience overwhelming feelings of guilt, isolation, grief, anger, depression, and shame. They often develop obsessive compulsive disorders and various forms of addictive behaviors such as eating disorders, and alcohol and drug abuse. Women find themselves having trouble bonding with their future husbands and children. They either become doting and controlling or detached and aloof. Women often feel alienated from God and from their faith community. At times they feel anger at God and a sense that they can never be forgiven.

Men often develop feelings of great guilt, remorse, sadness, and powerlessness. They often punish themselves by forms of self abuse such as alcoholism, drug use, or bodily mutilations (i.e., extensive piercings and tattoos). At times men can turn feelings of betrayal, powerlessness, and loss of trust into acts of aggression and abuse toward women. Men often seek to run away from these feelings by leaving their partners. It is not unusual that an abortion marks the end of a relationship.

Siblings of an aborted child—if they become aware of the abortion—are often afflicted by despair, confusion, and a general fear of the world. Because of repressed or subconscious anger, children of mothers who have had abortions have a higher rate of being physically abused. Siblings often suffer what is known as *Survivor Syndrome*, which is a mixture of anger and guilt associated with the overwhelming feeling of "why did I survive and my brother or sister didn't?" At times siblings feel that somehow their existence has caused the death of their sibling: "Mom and Dad could only handle one of us!" And in some cases children develop a paralyzing fear of their mothers, for they feel that "I might be next to get rid of."

The inability to bond, to sense love, leads to a rejection of God who is love. If a person cannot find a substitute for this love, even a heavenly substitute, as in the case of those who have embraced Mary as a substitute for their earthly mother, or Jesus or Joseph as a substitute for their earthly father, then a predisposition for atheism is produced.

More abortions, more post-abortion trauma, more atheism!

THE DEFECTIVE RELIGIOUS LEADER

Paul Vitz also makes the point that religious leaders, who are naturally father figures (as indicated by the title of *Father*, or *Reverend*) can distort the image of father by scandal, and thereby predispose people to atheism. A child who has been molested by a priest is not likely to be a person of faith.

Weak religious leaders also predispose people to atheism. A priest who is fearful of preaching against the evils of abortion, contraception, embryonic stem cell research, *in vitro* fertilization, homosexual activity, and on the other dimensions of the *culture of death,* is a priest not worthy of respect. If a priest cannot preach his convictions, *then these beliefs can't be that worthy of following.* Many are predisposed to atheism because of a lack of conviction by their priests or religious leaders.

John Toland, a deist or practical atheist, was the illegitimate child of a Catholic priest. He is reported to have burned *The Book of Common Prayer*, and would publish a work titled, *Christianity Not Mysterious.*[11]

Gandhi modeled his entire ministry on the *Beatitudes* of Jesus Christ. Yet, Gandhi never became a Christian. He once commented that he never became a Christian because he never met one. The Anglican ministers serving in India had failed to adequately protest the evils of British colonialism. They had failed to adequately model Christ.

Malcolm Muggeridge, on the other hand, a former, fervent atheist, was baptized into the Catholic Church. When asked why, he answered, "I encountered Jesus Christ." The puzzled onlookers asked him, "When did you see Jesus Christ?" He answered, "When I saw Mother Teresa of Calcutta I saw Jesus Christ!"

If a religious leader truly models what he or she believes, people are apt to model these leaders, and become believers.

THE SOPHISTICATED/RECOGNITION URGE

Low self-esteem often expresses itself in the desire for being recognized. Atheists often like to be seen as unique, sophisticated, as free-thinkers and rebels.

Paul Vetz explains: "Voltaire's ambition and intellectual vanity are agreed upon by all his biographers. His passion was for fame . . ."

Feuerbach has been described as a lonely figure whose loneliness "was the product of an unsatisfied intellectual vanity." He saw himself as a "philosopher of outstanding importance."[12]

Nietzsche's pride and his arrogance are widely acknowledged. Indeed, his philosophy is a celebration of this pride and arrogance. His obsession with power, with being a *superman*, with *killing God* exemplifies this innate need for recognition. Nietzsche supplanted Christ with himself. He often referred to himself as 'the Crucified One' — hardly a sign of modesty.

In his attempt to kill God, Nietzsche killed himself!

Sigmund Freud is often described by his biographers as ambitious, a trait best summarized in Freud's own statement about himself: "For I am actually not at all a man of science, not an observer, not an experimenter. . . . I am by temperament nothing but a conquistador (conqueror), an adventurer. . . ."[13]

Baron d'Holbach, a well-known atheist of the Enlightenment period, inflated his origins and bought his title of nobility. He rejected his father and mother, finding their social status as inadequate. Feeling unwanted by his parents, he sought to be wanted by his circle of friends, his "coterie" of "free-thinkers." Thus he found what he could not find in his parents, attention.[14]

John Toland, born illegitimately, sought to expunge his heritage. This led him to seek attention and even celebrity. He sought attention by associating with famous men like John Locke and by writing a shocking work, *Christianity Not Mysterious.*

Richard Carlyle, like Margaret Sanger, sought attention by advocating birth control at a time when birth control was viewed as pagan and unacceptable. He sought attention by writing radical letters to the press and by hungering for public attention.

Jill Johnston, who was abandoned by her father and distant from her mother, would express her dissatisfaction with life in her radical feminism and lesbianism. This would bring her the much needed attention she so much hungered for.

Carl Sagan sought to overcome what he perceived was his lower class upbringing—father a garment worker, mother a housewife.

The Marquis de Sade, known for being the "father of sadism" was completely devoid of any sexual limits. His biographers have described him as having an unconstrained desire for "grandeur." He was obsessed with shocking the world and gaining attention by his debauchery.[15]

Margaret Sanger, known for promoting birth control, abortion, and eugenics—the euthanizing of the "unfit"—always sought to be seen amongst the "enlightened and thoughtful."[16]

The media, particularly the movie and television industry, is made up of a disproportionate amount of practical atheists—the hunger for attention and fame being all-consuming.

BIRTH ORDER

Frank J. Sulloway in his book *Born to Rebel* has indicated that one's place within the birth order can have an impact on one's philosophical or intellectual belief system.[17] It is not unusual for younger children to be more rebellious and to seek their own ways. Younger children, seeking to assert their individuality and uniqueness, often resort to belief systems that will distinguish them from their siblings.

ATHEIST FATHER OR MOTHER HERO

Children, with loving and admirable fathers, will often embrace their father's faith system, whether theistic or atheistic. The father of John Stuart Mill, James Mill, is an example of this. John Stuart Mill's father was an accomplished and admired philosopher, historian and economist. He was a man devoted to his son, homeschooling him personally. The atheism of his father was adopted by the son as an act of love and admiration for his atheist father.[18]

Robert Taylor's father died when he was six years old. Robert was able to find a substitute father figure, his uncle. His uncle would advise Taylor to reject religion. In 1829 he would form a society dedicated to attacking and rejecting Christianity.

Simone de Beauvoir loved her father, who was a skeptic and unbeliever: "My father's skepticism had prepared the way for me; I would not be embarking alone upon a hazardous adventure. I even felt great relief at finding myself released from the bonds of my sex and my childhood."[19] Later in life, another hero would come into her life, Jean Paul Sartre: "My trust in him was so complete that he supplied me with the sort of absolute unfailing security that I had once had from my parents, or from God."[20]

Ayn Rand's father was a skeptic and promoter of individualism. The father's approval and admiration of his daughter gave significance to her life. She would model her belief system upon her father's.

What is said of fathers is equally valid of mothers.

ATHEISM—A PATHOLOGICAL RESPONSE TO SOCIAL DISINTEGRATION[21]

When societies begin to disintegrate, atheism often follows. As the sociologist Alexander Ross explains:

> [Man] relies heavily on the presence of society to provide a sense of purpose beyond himself. The loss of this presence, occasioned by the weakening of social bonds, so threatens his sense of meaning that he begins to entertain theories or systems of thought that corroborate his growing sense of meaninglessness. Such theories, by minimizing the transcendent importance of life, incline men to self-destruction [and to atheism].[22]

A society that embraces a communal, socially interactive spirit is one that fosters faith. Societies that have strong family structures, large families (three or more children), and two parent households foster faith in God. Societies that lack this necessary coherence are societies that birth atheism.[23]

God becomes replaced by the *security blanket* of science. As the sociologist Emile Durkheim explains, "[The] desire for learning is a result of the weakening of group attachments . . ."[24] The less people feel integrated into society, the more they turn to schooling. Learning is necessary for healthy growth, but *learning simply for learning* is the making of an idol to supplant a loss of faith in God.

Learning is a cry for meaning. Some find this meaning in the knowledge of God; others find their meaning in meaninglessness and materialism.

SUFFERING AND THE HERE AND NOW

The British scientist Alfred Russel Wallace gives an account of one of his experiments. While observing cocoons in which moths were developing, he noticed that one of the moths was beating its underdeveloped wing trying to break out of the cocoon. After seeing what he perceived was unbearable suffering, he decided to help the moth out of the cocoon. He took his knife, gently split the cocoon, and freed the moth. In the ensuing days, Russel noticed that the wings were not developing, the colors of the wings were absent, and the growth of the moth was stunted. It died several days later. Wallace realized that the struggle against the cocoon is what made the moth strong and capable of survival. It was in the struggle that the moth became stronger and more resilient.

To many, God does not exist because he cannot be found in the most tragic moments of life. They cry, "Why is the world in such a condition? Why does God allow disasters and so much suffering? Why is God so silent? Can a God who is love allow for so much suffering? Camus, while standing over the crushed body of a young boy turned to his friend and said while pointing to the sky, "You see, the sky is dumb." [25] Sam Harris' *Letter to a Christian Nation* would cry out: "An atheist is a person who believes that the murder of a single girl—even once in a million years—casts doubt upon the idea of a benevolent God."[26] Sam Harris' anger over 9/11 is also a mark of his atheism being based, in part, on his inability to grasp any significance in suffering.

Parents that lose a young child, or a husband or wife that loses a spouse often look for someone or something to blame. Incapable of dealing with the hurt they lash out at God—wanting to punish God. They repress God from their lives and their day to day living. They become practical atheists or in some cases categorical or militant atheists.

The fact remains, however, that only a God-based religion can bring about the necessary composure to assuage the sufferings of life. Even Karl Marx had to admit that. Marx knew the power of religion when he called it the opiate of the people. Atheists have not been able to find an answer to the problem of suffering, let alone a way of dealing with it.

Suffering is the unfortunate consequence of the misuse of free will. We have the free will to do good or the free will to do evil. That is, we can do that which is in harmony with our own nature, the nature of others, and the nature of creation in general, or we can do that which distorts this harmony. Harmony brings harmonious living, disharmony brings about suffering.

But what about the natural disasters that affect the world, and most particularly innocent lives? This particular aspect of suffering preoccupied most of St. Augustine of Hippo's life. After exhausting every possible theory he sought the Scriptures and found the doctrine of original sin. Original sin not only wounded the very nature of the person and his or her relationships, it also distorted the original harmony that was innate to creation. Due to this fracture in creation, due to the original misuse of freedom, evil persists.

The doctrine of original sin is correctly a matter of faith; however, it is the only explanation ever put forth in the history of the world that adequately explains the mystery of suffering in all its expressions.

God allows freedom because freedom is a requisite for love. We can choose to love God or not, but one way or the other we are choosing. The choices we make have a great impact on the kinds of people we become and the kind of world we help to create.

God did not make suffering something that could not be overcome. Rather he made it the means for perfecting our nature and keeping us aware of our priorities. Suffering is that which purifies the soul, sanctifies the person, and sets priorities in their proper order. Even Nietzsche had to admit, reluctantly, sarcastically, and bitterly, "What doesn't kill you is bound to make you better." God takes the trials and tribulations of life and transforms them into gifts, as numerous saints have attested to.

Change is necessary for personal growth, and change presupposes suffering, a dying to one's old ways and a rebirth into a new way of life. Without suffering there can be no personal growth of any significance.

Suffering is a teacher. It helps build compassion, empathy, self-mastery, endurance, patience, and courage. It helps to confirm our decision making processes and our knowledge of good and evil. It promotes interdependence and solidarity among people.

Life transcends the here and now. Life and relationships are eternal. This life here is but a *blink of the eye* when compared to eternity. True healing can only occur when a person, hindered by atheism, begins to comprehend this mystery.

Life is full of choices, full of world visions. Some seek to please God; some seek to please the world; some seek to rebel against it all!

Changing world visions is at the heart of healing the personality disorder of atheism.

The man who has not suffered cannot possibly know anything.
Rabbinic Saying

PERSONAL CONVENIENCE

Often people become atheists because they find it more convenient. Many seek the easy road in life. The American philosopher Mortimer Adler acknowledged that becoming religious "would require a radical change in my way of life, a basic alteration in the direction of day-to-day choices as well as in the ultimate objectives to be sought or hoped for. . . ."[27]

To be a believer in God is difficult, but to be an unbeliever is even more difficult. Mortimer Adler would eventually recognize this when in 1984 he was baptized into the Christian faith.

For others, however, there would be no conversion. Samuel Butler was a homosexual and did not want to be hindered by the morals of a God-based religion. He openly lived a hedonistic lifestyle. (Many homosexuals become atheists to justify an active homosexual lifestyle.)

Michel Onfray's affinity for hedonism finds justification in atheism.

Margaret Sanger, known for promoting birth control, abortion, and eugenics, was renowned for favoring open marriages and sexual promiscuity.

The Marquis de Sade's obsession with sadism, with sexual debauchery, was so intense that he would deny God and the morals of his time in order to satisfy his limitless sexual desires.

The pornography industry is made up of practical and militant atheists.

HARMFUL MUTATION/BIO-CHEMICAL THEORY

Mutations can be advantageous, disadvantageous, or indifferent. Many suffer from the *atheist personality disorder* because they have either a harmful mutation, or suffer from some bio-chemical imbalance. Atheism at first appears advantageous for survival since atheistic self-centeredness is beneficial in avoiding life-threatening situations. However, since atheism is incapable of authentic other-centeredness,[28] it is harmful for the good of society, which in turn is harmful to the individual. Therefore, other-centeredness is more beneficial for the survival of the species than self-centeredness. The inability to perceive in feeling or thought *transcendence* traps one into self-centeredness. This inability may be environmental and/or bio-chemical and/or a simple result of deficient evolution.[29]

Some have argued that malnutrition at childbirth, abnormal brain development, maternal alcoholism and/or drug abuse, and maternal anxiety—resulting in the detrimental release of hormones—have been responsible for a predilection toward atheism.[30]

ATHEISM'S "GOD"

We were created for God. If we do not find the true God we will find a substitute. The god of atheism is—for many—*science* and for others it is the *self* or *man*.

Science as god

What distinguishes us scientists from the pious and the believers is not the quality but the quantity of belief and piety; we are contented with less.[31]

Nietzsche

Since the sixteenth century the advances in the natural sciences have led, for many, to a conflict with philosophy and theology. The conviction that developed was that somehow knowledge and faith were irreconcilable. The more that was discovered in the field of the natural sciences the less God was needed.[32]

God was in their mindset a concept used to fill in the gaps of understanding (i.e., for Newton, God was the one who corrected the abnormalities in the orbits of the planets), but as science discovered plausible alternative explanations the need for God was less apparent.

The *New Atheists* Richard Dawkins, Daniel Dennett, Christopher Hitchens, and Sam Harris are worshipers of this religion of science.[33] In the words of Hitchens: "[All] attempts to reconcile faith with science and reason are consigned to failure and ridicule."[34] For Feuerbach, belief in God is a pre-scientific mode of thought. For Dawkins, as for Marx, the world must be exclusively understood in terms of materialism: "Our programme is based entirely on the scientific—to be more precise—upon a materialist world conception."[35] Religion is a fog to knowledge. For Richard Dawkins, the goal is to kill God-based religions so that the god of science may reign.[36]

For atheists, science is god and is interpreted through the *scriptures* of an atheistic version of Darwinism. The exercise of freedom is seen as freedom from restraint, not freedom to do good, for good is relative.

Atomic and nuclear bombs, lethal genetic and chemical weapons, designer babies, cloning, embryonic stem cell research, radioactive waste, global warming, pollution, etc., become a possibility when science becomes god. Without a proper religion of stewardship, science can go amuck. The Tuskegee Syphilis Experiment resulted in the forced sterilization of 64,000 people—science gone amuck. The *Atlas of Topographical and Applied Human Anatomy* was created by the dissection of 1,377 Gestapo Nazi concentration camp victims.[37]

Man as god

Atheists are inherently rebellious. This rebellious nature expresses itself in a misguided notion of personal freedom and autonomy. The development of atheism in the name of this misguided notion of personal freedom and autonomy is found in most atheists, including the legendary atheists such as Ludwig Feuerbach, Sigmund Freud and Karl Marx. Friedrich Nietzsche saw the consequences of such a secular notion of the world.[38]

Ludwig Feuerbach developed a theory of projection to explain belief in God—which was later enhanced and made famous by Freud. For Feuerbach and his followers, belief in God is nothing other than the projection and objectification of a person's own being, and nothing more.[39]

> *Man makes a god of what he is not but would like to be; that is his god. A Christian would like to be perfect, free from sin, without bodily needs, divine, immortal and blissful, but he is not; he therefore conceives of a being who is what he himself would like to be and hopes to become some day. . . .*[40]

> *The beginning, middle, and end of religion is man.*[41]

For Feuerbach, the human person is not able to find fulfillment in himself (herself) and thus he (she) projects this desire for fulfillment, for infinity, unto God. What the person would like to be is what he or she projects unto his or her belief in God. But by doing this, the person alienates and estranges himself or herself from his or her true fulfillment. One becomes empty by denying oneself what one projects unto God. The belief in God, it is argued, has the negative characteristic of alienating the person from his or her own nature. The way to get out of this dilemma, for Feuerbach, is to say *no* to God, and by saying *no* to God one says *yes* to one's humanity.[42]

Building upon the work of Feuerbach, Karl Marx, like Feuerbach, asserted that the belief in God was simply a projection and therefore a creation of the person. For Marx *the human person is the Supreme Being, the redeemer of himself or herself, the root of himself or herself.* For Marx, one is created by oneself and for oneself. Atheism becomes the liberator of the person by freeing the person from one's delusions. A humanism separated from belief in God becomes the way to fulfillment and meaningful living.[43]

For Karl Marx, however, unlike for Feuerbach, a God-based religion is not the projection of the person's self-consciousness *per se* as much as it is the projection of the world's consciousness. A God-based religion is the sigh of the oppressed creature, the sentiment of a heartless world, and the soul of soulless conditions. It is the *opium of the people.*[44]

A God-based religion is that which brings consolation to a life of difficulty. The belief in God is the necessary consequence of inequality in material relationships. If these conditions which bring about the development of belief in God are changed (i.e., inequality) then belief in God will die out through a natural process.[45] Marx believes in a *utopian man* and a *utopian society.*

For Marx, belief in God will disappear because it deals in an illusion of happiness. Once the conditions of possibility for the illusion disappear the person will be able to free himself (herself) and control his (her) own destiny, his (her) own happiness and meaning, his (her) own reality. When the relationships between people and between people and nature are organized into relationships that are intelligible and reasonable, then a God-based religion will no longer be needed as an opiate. Then the human person will be truly liberated, truly free, and fully human.[46]

The works of Feuerbach and Marx fathered Friedrich Nietzsche. Nietzsche renounced metaphysics by denying the idea of absolutes, such as absolute truth. For Nietzsche a *yes* to God is the same as a *no* to life. The consequences of atheism for Nietzsche is the death of God and the new dawn of the *superman*, the ultimate perfected being of evolution.[47]

Everything that has hitherto been called 'truth' has been recognized as the most harmful, insidious, and subterranean form of lie; the holy pretext of 'improving' mankind as the ruse of sucking the blood of life itself. Morality as moral vampirism. . . . The concept of 'God' invented as a counter concept of life—everything harmful, poisonous, slanderous, the whole hostility unto death against life synthesized in this concept in a gruesome unity! The concept of 'beyond,' the 'true world' invented in order to devaluate the only world there is—in order to retain no goal, no reason, no task for our earthly reality! The concept of the 'soul' the 'spirit,' finally even 'immortal soul,' invented in order to despise the body, to make it sick, 'holy' . . . Escrasez L'infame![48]

For Feuerbach, Marx, and Nietzsche (and the proponents of the *New Athe-ism*) a God-based religion robs one of one's integrity and transfers one's energies and responsibilities to another world projected by one's own misguided and deceived perceptions.[49]

The theory of projection, despite its use by atheists, in no way affirms or denies the existence of God. Projecting into something other (i.e., another human being or *thing*) does not prove or disprove the existence or non-existence of God.

The theory of projection is simply a natural human psychological process that seeks to comfort or assuage one's innate needs and desires. We often hate in others what we hate in ourselves; we often observe in others those characteristics that we recognize in ourselves. This process is sometimes conscious but most often it is found at the subconscious level.

Many are attracted to stardom, and even serial killing, out of a need to have their names known beyond their life-spans—a form of immortality. Many a conqueror has sought their immortality through conquests. Freud viewed himself, as earlier cited, as a conqueror.

For the atheist, one's needs and wishes are projected into something other than *god*. If a person sees himself as unsophisticated or uneducated or suffering from a low self-esteem, the person is likely, at the conscious or subconscious level, to find atheism as very attractive for it makes one seem unique, sophisticated, respected, esteemed, intellectual, and even high class. If the intellectual fad of the period is atheism, then such a person is prone to embracing the fad that is in vogue.

For other atheists the need to comfort and assuage one's needs and wishes are projections upon something other than the self such as science.

For others one's needs and desires are projected upon a utopian society (i.e., Marx) with the hope that a perfect or near perfect society will eliminate our need for a *god*—that lasting happiness will be attainable in the here and now without God.

Implied in the deification of science, and the atheist's understanding of the theory of projection is a deep seated, often subconscious, desire to be a *super-man*, a *utopian man*. Implicit in this utopian concept of man is the belief that cultural and biological evolution will in time make all knowledge accessible to the human mind. Man will truly be a god! Darwin's dream of a utopian society reflects this belief:

> *The view now held by most physicists is that the sun with all the planets will in time grow too cold for life, unless some great body dashes into the sun and thus gives it fresh life. . . . Believing as I do that man in the distant future will be a far more perfect creature than he is now, it is an intolerable thought that*

he and all other sentient beings are doomed to complete annihilation after such long-continued slow progress.[50]

For atheists science or man is god, or in the process of becoming a god. The idea that there could be a *superior mind*, God, is not within the scope of atheism's paradigm.

The theory of projection is a coping mechanism that allows one to cope with the vicissitudes of life. Psychological theories such as the theory of projection are *ad hominem* arguments: Or as the renowned psychologists Paul Vitz explains, "[These forms of arguments] address the person presenting the evidence and not the evidence itself." [51]

One thing we can all agree upon is that the theory of projection can be helpful in the growth of self-awareness or self-knowledge.

For God-believers it can be a purifying method for spiritual growth. As Vitz remarks: "In short, the psychological critique provided by atheism can be a valuable reminder and help to believers in their struggle to avoid worshipping a mere projection of the self—a kind of psychological idol."[52]

To explain away the existence of God, one needs to have a structure of reasoning that will allow for this. One needs to supplant God with the *self* or with *science*.

IN CONCLUSION

The topic of atheism is one that has fascinated me since my first reading of Nietzsche. It is a topic that would become the source of my master's thesis and my first book. It is now eleven years later, and I find myself more fascinated than ever.

NOTES

1. I am indebted to the pioneering work of Paul C. Vitz, The Faith of the Fatherless: The Psychology of Atheism (Dallas: Spence Publishing, Co., 1999) for this section. His theory and biographical information were essential to this work. Other sources worthy of study: B. Malinowski, The Father in Primitive Psychology (New York: Norton, 1927); J. MacMurray, Persons in Relation, vol. 8 (Highlands: Humanities Press, 1961); David Blankenhorn, Fatherless America (New York: Basic Books, 1995); Benedict Groeschel, Spiritual Passages (New York: Crossroads, 1983). Cases studies in practical atheism are found in Time Warner's compilation Born to be Killers: The Complexity of Abnormal Human Behavior, 2006.

2. Cf. A.M. Rizzuto, The Birth of the Living God (Chicago: University of Chicago Press, 1979); J.W. Jones, Contemporary Psychoanalysis and Religion (New Haven: Yale University Press, 1991); M. H. Spero, Religious Objects as Psychological Structures (Chicago: University of Chicago Press, 1992) W.W. Meissner, Psychoanalysis and Religious Experience (New Haven: Yale University Press, 1984); Robert Campbell, Campbell's Psychiatric Dictionary (Oxford: Oxford University Press, 2003); Andrew Coleman, ed., A Dictionary of Psychology (Oxford: Oxford University Press, 2007); Graham Davey, ed., Encyclopaedic Dictionary of Psychology (Oxford: Oxford University Press, 2005).

3. Sigmund Freud, Leonardo da Vinci (New York: Random House, 1947), 98.

4. Ronald Hayman, Nietzsche: A Critical Life (New York: Oxford University Press, 1980), 18.

5. Deists are practical atheists—they live life as if God did not exist.

6. Cf. Case studies of Paul Vitz in Faith of the Fatherless.

7. W.J. Murray, My Life Without God (Nashville: Thomas Nelson, 1982), 7.

8. Cf. Vitz, 121–122.

9. Cf. Vitz, 119.

10. D. Wiener, Albert Ellis: Passionate Skeptic (New York: Praeger, 1998), 7–42.

11. R.E. Sullivan, John Toland and the Deist Controversy (Cambridge: Harvard University Press, 1982).

12. Ibid.

13. Ibid.

14. A.C. Kors, D'Holbach's Coterie (Princeton: Princeton University Press, 1976), 158.

15. Cf. Encyclopedia Britannica, vol. 19, 1971.

16. Margaret Sanger, The Pivot of Civilization, edited by Michael Perry (Seattle: Inkling Books, 2001), Preface.

17. Frank Sulloway, Born to Rebel: Birth Order: Family Dynamic and Creative Lives (New York: Pantheon, 1996).

18. Ibid., 108. Cf. Paul Vitz.

19. Simone de Beauvoir, Memoirs of a Dutiful Daughter, trans. J. Kirkup (Cleveland: World Publishing, 1959), 145.

20. S.L. Archer, "Gender Differences in Identity Development," Journal of Adolescence 12 (1989): 25.

21. Cf. G. Alexander Ross, "Spiritual Suicide," The Catholic Social Science Review VIII (2003),: 2007–222.

22. Cf. Ibid., Alexander Ross, Abstract of "Spiritual Suicide," 2.

23. Ibid., 1–11.

24. Emile Durkheim, Suicide: A Study of Sociology, trans. John A. Spaulding (New York: Free Press, 1951), 209.

25. Cf. Ibid, 31, 137.

26. Sam Harris, Letter to a Christian Nation (New York: Knopf, 2006), 51.

27. Mortimer Adler, Philosopher at Large (New York: Macmillan, 1977), 316.

28. Some atheists are capable of philanthropy and altruism, but it is rare. Most often atheists practice deficient altrusm. Those who suffer from dependent personality disorders are very much focused on the good of others, but only to the extent that it affects the person with the disorder.

29. Such people are not excluded from salvation. Damnation requires freedom and knowledge. Those impacted by this disorder are hindered in their freedom and knowledge; thus, the possibility of salvation.

30. Adapted and built upon the research of John Bowlby, The Making and Breaking of Affectional Bonds, 1979.

31. Nietzsche, Assorted Opinions and Maxims, s. 98, trans. R.J. Hollingdale.

32. The theology of the deification of science is explicated in John Pasquini, Atheism and Salvation (Lanham: University Press of America, 2000), 27–28: Basic Writings of Nietzsche, ed. and trans. Walter Kaufmann (New York: The Modern Library, 1992), 269.

33. Dawkins, The God Delusion, 18, 84, 98, 284; Dennett, Breaking the Spell, 47; Sam Harris, Letter to a Christian Nation, 63.

34. Christopher Hitchens, god is not Great, (New York: Twelve), 64–65.

35. Marx, On Religion, 9.

36. "Against Ignorance: Science Education in the 21st Century—A Conversation with Richard Dawkins and Lawrence Krauss," Aurora Forum at Stanford University, March 9, 2008.

37. Cf. Vox Day.

38. Pasquini, Atheism and Salvation, 28; Buckley, Atheism, 56.

39. For Freud the religion of Christianity became in his mind replaced by the religion of psychotherapy.

40. Ludwig Feuerbach, Lectures on the Essence of Religion, trans. Ralph Manheim, New York: Harper and Row Publishers, 1967, 234). Feuerbach would eventually drop a great part of his theory of projection, after much intellectual criticism. He would spend his later years working on the person's innate hunger for immortality and the conquering of death. Feuerbach's work would continually evolve under criticism, and in the end would never fully overcome much of its philosophical contradictions (cf. Stanford Encyclopedia of Philosophy).

41. Ludwig Feuerbach, The Essence of Christianity, trans. George Eliot (New York: Harper and Row, 1957), 184.

42. Pasquini, Atheism and Salvation, 29.

43. Cf. Walter Kasper, The God of Jesus Christ, trans. Matthew J. O'Connell (New York: Crossroad Publishing, 1992), 29–37.

44. Karl Marx, "Contribution to the Critique of Hegel's Philosophy of Right, quoted in Walter Kasper, The God of Jesus Christ (New York: Crossroad Publishing, 1992), 37, n. 98.

45. Christopher Hitchens expresses an affinity to this utopian idea of the future without a God-religion in god is not Great, 283.

46. Pasquini, Atheism and Salvation, 30.

47. Dagobert Runes, ed., Dictionary of Philosophy (Savage: Littlefield, Inc., 1983), 323.

48. Walter Kaufmann, ed. and trans. Basic Writings of Nietzsche (New York: Random House, 1968), 790–791.

49. Cf. Charles Moeller, "The Theology of Unbelief," Concilium: Theology in the Age of Renewal 23 (February 1967): 35.

50. Charles Darwin, The Autobiography of Charles Darwin, ed. N. Barlow (New York: Harcourt Brace, 1959), 92.

51. Paul C. Vitz, The Faith of the Fatherless, 145.

52. Ibid. 144–145.

Appendix II

Hope for the Hopeless:[1]
A Catholic Perspective

Not all atheists are the same. Atheists, even if they are unaware, are confronted with God, and for some, even despite themselves, will be saved by God's infinite mercy.[2]

The Catholic Church affirms that Christ is the way and the truth and the life and that no one goes to the Father except through the Son (Jn. 14:6), and consequently through his Body, his Bride, the Church. All salvation therefore comes from Christ and his Body the Church (1 Cor. 12:12f; 2 Cor. 11:2; Rom. 12:5; Eph. 1:22f; 5:25, 27; Rev. 19:7). Faith, which implies holy works, baptism,[3] and consequently the Church are necessary for salvation.

How does the atheist fit in here? Some are atheists through and through. Some atheists are atheistic in mind but not in soul. An atheism that is held *through no fault of the person*, allows for salvation.

> *Those who, through no fault of their own, do not know the Gospel of Christ or his Church, but who nevertheless seek God with a sincere heart, and, moved by grace, try in their actions to do his will as they know it through the dictates of their conscience--those too may achieve eternal salvation (LG 16).*

One who is authentically holy is one who has the gift of grace at the core of his or her being. And since Christ is another word for grace, Christ consequently is the source of salvation for a person of authentic holiness, whether that person is explicitly aware of it or not. Such a person is saved by Christ who is the way and the truth and the life and that person is brought to the Father through the Son (Jn. 14:6). The soul of such a person is one in which *implicit* faith is being experienced. Such a soul makes one a member of the Mystical Body of Christ, the Church, through an implicit baptism of desire into the mystery which is Christ.

This reality finds its most beautiful expression in Matthew 25:

> *Just as you did it to one of the least of my brethren, you did it to me. . . . Come,*
> *you blessed by my Father inherit the kingdom prepared for you from the founda-*
> *tion of the world; for I was hungry and you gave me something to drink, I was*
> *a stranger and you welcomed me, I was naked and you gave me clothing, I was*
> *sick and you took care of me, I was in prison and you visited me.*

Or in the words of St. Anselm:

> *When we speak about wisdom, we are speaking of Christ. When we speak about*
> *virtue, we are speaking of Christ. When we speak about justice, we are speak-*
> *ing of Christ. When we speak about peace, we are speaking of Christ. When we*
> *speak about truth and life . . ., we are speaking of Christ.*[4]

Never lose hope, for Christ is the hope for the hopeless.[5] If a person follows
one's conscience, then one is following the call of grace, and grace is another
word for Christ, another word for a baptism of desire, another word for salvation. The mind may be atheistic, but the soul *may* not be!

IN CONCLUSION

The birth of the *New Atheists* has brought about the birth of the *New Theists*.
We owe much to the *New Atheists* for in their denials they have validated
more than ever, perhaps more than ever in the history of the world, the existence of God!

NOTES

1. CCC 846–856.
2. cf. Rahner, *Theological Investigations*, vol. 9, 15 5–156; John Pasquini, *Atheism
and Salvation* (Lanham: University Press of America, 2000), 40–43.
3. Baptism by desire found in Pasquini, *Atheism and Salvation*, 77–87.
4. Psalms. 36, 6 5–66: CSEL 64,12 3–124.
5. John Pasquini, *Light, Happiness, and Peace* (New York: Alba House, 2004),
159–163; Ibid., *Ecce Fides* (Indiana: S of C Publications, 2007), 156–158.

Epilogue

Microevolution is a fact of life. Macroevolution however is not. Traditional Darwinism, and even Neo-Darwinism, is a theory in crisis. While a great part of the world has no trouble seeing this, the Anglo-Saxon world is still fervently and uncompromisingly Darwinistic.

When arguing for the existence of God one has to argue on the playing field of one's opponents. And so I have.

But the reality remains, if evolution at the macro level is proved to be a fraud, then atheism has no intellectual ground to stand upon. God becomes fact! If macroevolution is a fact, then it is only so because God made it so, for, as scientist have proven—particularly molecular biologists and astronomers—chance, randomness, and natural selection will never be able to adequately explain the reality in which we live.

Bibliography

Anderson, B. W., *Understanding the Old Testament* (4th Ed.; EC: Prentice Hall, 1986).

Adkins, Lesley. *Dictionary of Roman Religions.* Oxford: Oxford University Press, 2000.

Aldridge, O. *Voltaire and the Century of Light.* Princeton: Princeton University Press, 1975.

Aquinas, Thomas. *Summa Theologiae.* Translated by Timothy McDermott. Westminster: Christian Classics, 1989.

Ashely, Benedict. *Health Care Ethics.* Washington: Georgetown University Press, 1997.

Bachmann, Talis. *The Experimental Phenomena of Consciousness.* Oxford: Oxford University Press, 2007.

Baker, Daniel. *Explorers and Discovers of the World.* Washington: Gale Research, 1993.

Baldwin, John. *The Scholastic Culture of the Middle Ages.* Lexington: D.C. Heath, 1971.

Baluffi, Cajetan. *The Charity and the Church.* Dublin: Gill and Son, 1885.

Barro, Robert. "Which Countries Have State Religions?" Harvard University, 2005.

Bary, William ed., *Introduction to Oriental Civilizations.* Vol. 1. *Sources of Chinese Tradition.* New York: Columbia University Press, 1963.

Behe, Michael, William Dembski and Stephen Meyer. *The Proceedings of the Wethersfied Institute: Science and Evidence for Design in the Universe.* San Francisco: Ignatius Press, 1999.

Behe, Michael. *The Edge of Evolution.* New York: Free Press, 2006.

Bergant, Dianne. ed., *The Collegeville Bible Commentary.* Collegeville: The Liturgical Press, 1988.

Berman, Harold. *Faith and Order: The Reconciliation of Law and Religion.* Atlanta: Scholars Press, 1993.

———. *Law and Revolution.* Cambridge: Harvard University Press, 1983.

Betham, Jeremy. *An Introduction to the Principles of Morals and Legislation*. New York: Hafner, 1948.

Blankenhorn, David. *Fatherless America*. New York: Basic Books, 1995.

Boadt, L., *Reading the Old Testament: An Introduction*. New York: Paulist Press, 1984.

Bohlander, Richard. *World Explorers and Discovers*. New York: Macmillan, 1992.

Bondanella Peter. *The Portable Machiavelli*. New York: Vintage, 1994.

Bowker, John. *The Concise Oxford Dictionary of World Religions*. Oxford: Oxford University Press, 2005.

Boyd, Gregory. *God at War: The Bible and Spiritual Conflict*. Downers Grove: InterVarsity Press, 1997.

Brantl, George. ed., *Catholicism*. New York: George Braziller, Inc., 1961.

Brown, Raymond. ed., *The New Jerome Biblical Commentary*. Englewood Cliffs: Prentice Hall, 1988.

Brzezinski, Zbigniew. *Out of Control*. New York: Touchstone, 1995.

Buckley, Michael. *At the Origins of Modern Atheism*. New Haven: Yale University Press, 1979.

Burke, Theresa. *Forbidden Grief*. Springfield: Acorn Books, 2002.

Burkert, Walter. *Ancient Mystery Cults*. Cambridge: Harvard University Press, 1987.

Butterfield, Herbert. *The Origins of Modern Science*. New York: Free Press, 1957.

Cahill, Thomas. *How the Irish Saved Civilization*. New York: Doubleday, 1995.

Campbell, Robert. *Campbell's Psychiatric Dictionary*. Oxford: Oxford University Press, 2003.

Camus, Albert. *The First Man*. New York: Knopf, 1995.

Cary, Max. *The Ancient Explorers*. London: Methuen, 1929.

Clark, Kenneth. *Civilization: A Personal View*. New York: HarperPerennial, 1969.

Clowes, Brian. *The Facts of Life*. Front Royal: HLI, 2001.

Coban, A. B. *The Medieval Universities: Their Development and Organization*. London: Methuen and Co., 1975.

Cole, Susan. *Theo Mgaloi*. Leiden: Brill, 1984.

Coleman, Andrew. ed., *A Dictionary of Psychology*. Oxford: Oxford University Press, 2007.

Coleman, Gerald. *Human Sexuality: An All-Embracing Gift*. New York: Alba, 1992.

Collins, Francis. "Faith and the Human Genome." *Perspectives on Science and Christian Faith*. Vol. 55. 2003: 152.

Comstock, G. *Television in America*. Newbury Park: Sage Publications, 1991.

Crick, Francis. *The Astonishing Hypothesis: The Scientific Search for the Soul*. New York: Touchtone, 1995.

———. *What Mad Pursuit*. New York: Basic Books, 1988.

Daly, Lowrie. *The Medieval University*. New York: Sheed and Ward, 1961.

Daniel-Rop, Henri. *The Church in the Dark Ages*. New York: MJF Books, 1950.

Darwin, Charles. *The Autobiography of Charles Darwin*. New York: Harcourt Brace, 1959.

———. *The Descent of Man*. Princeton: Princeton University Press, 1981.

——. *On the Origins of Species.* Cambridge: Harvard University Press, 1964.

Davey, Graham. ed., *Encyclopaedic Dictionary of Psychology.* Oxford: Oxford University Press, 2005.

Dawkins, Richard. *The Blind Watchmaker.* New York: W.W. Norton and Company, 2006.

——. *The God Delusion.* London: Bantam Press, 2006.

——. *The Selfish Gene.* Oxford: Oxford University Press, 2006.

——. *Unweaving the Rainbow.* Boston: Mariner, 1998.

Dawson, Christopher. *Religion and the Rise of Western Culture.* New York: Image Books, 1991.

Davis, Michael. *For Altar and Throne.* St. Paul: Remnant, 1997.

Day, Vox. *The Irrational Atheist.* New York: Benbella, 2008.

Degler. Carl. *In Search of Human Nature.* New York: Oxford University Press, 1991.

Diamant, Anita. "Media Violence." *Parents.* October 1994: 40–45.

Descartes, Rene. *Rules for the Direction of the Mind.* Vol. 2. *The Philosophical Writings of Descartes.* Edited and Translated by J. Cottingham. Cambridge: Cambridge University Press, 1994.

——. *The World.*, Ibid.

——. *Principles of Philosophy.*, Ibid.

——. *The Passions of the Soul.*, Ibid.

——. *Meditations on First Philosophy.*, Vol. 2., Ibid. Oxford: Oxford University Press, 1984.

Dembski, William. *The Design Inference.* Cambridge: Cambridge University Press, 1998.

——. *The Design of Life.* Dallas: Foundations for Thought and Ethics, 2007.

——. *Understanding Intelligent Design.* Eugene: Harvest House Publishers, 1995.

Dennett, Daniel. *Breaking the Spell.* New York: Penguin Books, 2007.

——. *Consciousness Explained.* London: Penguin Books, 2004.

——. *Darwin's Dangerous Idea.* London: Penguin Books, 2007.

——. *Freedom Evolves.* London: Penguin Books, 2004.

Denton, Michael. *Evolution: A Theory in Crisis.* Chevy Chase: Adler and Adler, 1986.

DeVaux, R. *Ancient Israel.* New York: McGraw-Hill, 1961.

Egan, Harvey. *An Anthology of Christian Mysticism.* Minnesota: The Liturgical Press, 1991.

Eissfeldt, O., *The Old Testament: An Introduction.* New York: Harper, 1965.

Encyclopedia of Catholic History. ed., Mathew Bunson. Huntington: OSV, 2004.

Ferguson, John. *The Religions of the Roman Empire.* Ithaca: Cornell University Press, 1970.

Feuerbach, Ludwig. *The Essence of Christianity.* Translated by George Eliot. New York: Harper and Row Publishers, 1957.

——. *Lectures on the Essence of Christianity.* Translated by Ralph Manheim. New York: Harper and Row Publishers, 1967.

——. *Lectures on the Essence of Religion.* Translated by Ralph Manheim. New York: Harper and Row Publishers, 1967.

Finley, M.I. *The Portable Greek Historians*. New York: Penguin Books, 1982.

Fitzmyer, J.A., *An Introductory Bibliography for the Study of Scripture* (Subsidia biblica 3; Rome: Biblical Institute, 1981).

Flew, Antony. *There is a God: How the World's Most Notorious Atheist Changed His Mind*. New York: HarperOne, 2008.

———. "My Pilgrimage from Atheism to Theism." *Philosophia Christi*. Vol. 6. 2004: 201.

Freud, Sigmund. *The Future of an Illusion*. Translated by J. Strachey. New York: Norton, 1961.

———. *Civilizations and its Discontents*. Translated by J. Strachey. New York: Norton, 1961.

———. *Ego and the Id*. Edited and Translated by J. Strachey. New York: Norton, 1962.

———. *Leonardo da Vinci*. New York: Random House, 1947.

———. *Totem and Taboo*. Translated by J. Strachey. New York: Norton, 1950.

Friedrich, Gerhard. ed., *Theological Dictionary of the New Testament*. Grand Rapids: Eerdmanns, 1988.

Gaffney, James. *Moral Questions*. New York: Paulist Press, 1974.

Gallaher, John. *Time Past, Time Future: An Historical Study of Catholic Moral Theology*. New York: Paulist Press, 1990.

———. *The Basis for Christian Ethics*. New York: Paulist Press, 1985.

Genovesi, Vincent. *In Pursuit of Love: Catholic Morality and Human Sexuality*. Collegeville: The Liturgical Press, 1996.

Gibbon, Edward. *The Decline and Fall of the Roman Empire*. Vols. 1–III. New York: The Modern Library.

Gimpel, Jean. *The Medieval Machine*. New York: Holt, Rinehart, and Winston, 1976.

Girardi, Jules. "Reflections on Religious Indifference." *Concillium: Theology in the Age of Renewal* 23 (February 1967): 60–69.

Goldwin, Joscelyn. *Mystery Religion in the Ancient World*. Ithaca: Cornell University Press, 1971.

Gould, Stephen. *Wonderful Life*. New York: Norton, 1989.

———. "Evolution's Erratic Pace." *Natural History*. Vol. 86. May 1977: 199–208.

Grant, Neil. *The Discoverers*. New York: Arco Publishing, 1979.

Gregoire, Reginald. *The Monastic Realm*. New York: Rizzoli, 1985.

Groeschel, Benedict. *Spiritual Passages*. New York: Crossroads, 1983.

Gula, Richard. *Reason Informed by Faith: Foundations of Catholic Morality*. New York: Paulist Press, 1988.

Hanke, Lewis. *All Mankind is One*. DeKalb: Northern Illinois University Press, 1974.

Harmon, Gilbert. *Moral Relativism and Moral Objectivity*. New York: Blackwell, 1996.

Harring, Bernard. *Morality is for Persons: the Ethics of Christian Personalism*. New York: Farrar, Straus and Giroux, 1971.

Harris, Sam. *The End of Faith*. New York: W.W. Norton and Company, 2004.

——. *Letter to a Christian Nation.* New York: Alfred A. Knopf, 2006.

Hauser, Marc. *How Nature Designed Our Universal Sense of Right and Wrong.* New York: HarperCollins, 2006.

Hayman, Ronald. *Nietzsche: A Critical Life.* New York: Oxford University Press, 1980.

Hegel, G.W.F. *The Essential Writings.* Edited and Translated by Frederick Weiss. New York: Harper and Row, 2001.

——. *The Ethics of Hegel.* Edited and Translated by J. MacBride Sterrett. Boston: Ginn, 1993.

Heilbron, J. L. Annual Invitation Lecture to the Scientific Instrument Society. Royal Institution, London, December 6, 1995.

Hentz, Otto. "Foundations of Christian Faith: An Introduction in the Idea of Christianity." *Thought: A Review of Culture and Ideas* LIII (December 1978): 433–441.

Herrmann. S., *A History of Israel in Old Testament Times.* Second Edition. Philadelphia: Fortress, 1981.

Hitchens, Christorpher. *god is not Great.* New York: Twelve, 2007.

Hobbes, Thomas. *Leviathan.* ed., J.C.A. Gaskin. Oxford: Oxford University Press, 1962.

——. *On the Citizen.* ed., Richard Tuck. Cambridge: Cambridge University Press, 1998.

Hume, David. *A Treatise on Human Nature.* ed., L. A. Selby-Bigge. Oxford: Clarendon Press, 1978.

——. *Enquiries Concerning Human Understanding and Concerning Principles of Morals*, Ibid.

——. *The Natural History of Religion and Dialogues concerning Natural Religion*, ed., Wayne Colver. Ibid., 1976.

——. *Essays, Moral, Political, and Literary.* ed., Eugene Miller. Indianapolis: Liberty Classics, 1985.

Jaki, Stanley. *The Savior and Science.* Grand Rapids: Eerdmans, 200.

Jones, W.J. *Contemporary Psychoanalysis and Religion.* New Haven: Yale University Press, 1991.

Kamen, Henry. *The Spanish Inquisition: A Historical Revision.* New Haven: Yale University Press, 1997.

Kant, Immanuel. *Critique of Pure Reason.* Translated by Max Muller. New York: McMillan Co., 1966.

Kasper, Walter. *The God of Jesus Christ.* Translated by Matthew J. O'Connell. New York: Crossroad Publishing Co., 1992.

Kasun, Jacqueline. *War Against Population.* San Francisco: Ignatius Press, 1999.

Kaufmann, Walter, ed. and trans. *Basic Writings of Nietzsche.* New York: Random House, Inc., 1968.

Knowles, David. *The Evolution of Medieval Thought.* Second Edition. London: Longman, 1988.

Koerbel, Pam. *Abortions Second Victim.* Wheaton: Victor Books, 1986.

Kummel, E.G., *Introduction to the New Testament.* Nashville: Abingdon, 1975.

Langford, Jerome. *Galileo, Science, and the Church.* New York: Desclee, 1966.

Lecky, William. *History of European Morals.* Vol. 1. New York: Appleton, 1870.

Lynch, Joseph. *The Medieval Church.* London: Longman, 1992.

MacDonell, Joseph. *Jesuit Geometers.* St. Louis: Institute of Jesuit Sources, 1989.

MacMurray, J. *Persons in Relation.* Atlantic Highlands: Humanities Press, 1961.

Mahoney, John. *The Making of Moral Theology: A Study of Roman Catholic Tradition.* Oxford: Clarenton Press, 1987.

Malenowski, B. *The Father in Primitive Psychology.* New York: Norton, 1927.

Mortimer, Adler. *Philosopher at Large.* New York: Macmillan, 1977.

Martindale, C.C. *The Message of Fatima.* New York: London, Burns and Oates, 1950.

Marx, Karl. *On Religion.* Edited and Translated by Saul Padover. New York: McGraw Hill, 1974.

McCool, Gerald. *The Neo-Thomists.* Milwaukee: Marquette University Press, 1994.

Mendel, Arthur. *Essential Works of Marxism.* New York: Bantam, 1963.

Meissner, W.W. *Psychoanalysis and Religious Experience.* New Haven: Yale University Press, 1984.

Metzger, Bruce. ed., *The Oxford Companion to the Bible.* Oxford: Oxford University Press, 1988.

Meyer, Marvin. ed., *Sacred Texts of the Mystery Religions.* Philadelphia: University of Pennsylvania Press, 1999.

Mill, John Stuart. *Utilitarianism.* Englewood Cliffs: Prentice Hall, 1957.

Miller, J.M., *A History of Ancient Israel and Judah.* Philadelphia: Westminster, 1986.

Milton, Richard. *Shattering the Myths of Darwinism.* Rochester: Park Street Press, 1997.

Moeller, Charles. "Theology and Unbelief." *Concilium: Theology in the Age of Renewal* 23 (February 1967): 25–46.

Moleswworth, William. ed., *The English Works of Thomas Hobbes.* Oxford: Oxford University Press, 1962.

Mortimer, Jeffery. "How TV Violence Hits Kids." *The Education Digest.* October 1994: 16–19.

Muck, Otto. *The Transcendental Method.* Translated by William D. Seidensticker. New York: Herder and Herder, 1968.

O'Connor, John. *Monasticism and Civilization.* New York: Kennedy and Sons, 1921.

O'Leary, Denyse. *By Design or by Chance.* Minneapolis: Augsburg, 2004.

Opie, Iona. *A Dictionary of Superstitions.* Oxford: Oxford University Press, 2005.

Neuner, J. and J. Dupuis, eds. *The Christian Faith: In the Doctrinal Documents of the Catholic Church.* New York: Alba House, 1990.

Newman, John Cardinal Henry. *An Essay in Aid of a Grammar of Ascent.* Westminster: Christian Classics, 1973.

——. *Essays and Sketches.* Vol. 3. New York: Longmans, Green and Co., 1948.

Nietzsche, Friedrich. *Beyond Good and Evil.* Translated by Walter Kaufmann. New York: Vintage, 1966.

——. *Ecce Homo.* Translated by R. J. Hollingdale. London: Penguin, 1979.

———. *Selected Letters of Friedrich Nietzsche*. Translated by C. Middleton. Chicago: University of Chicago Press, 1969.

———. *Basic Writings of Nietzsche*. New York: Random House, 1968.

North, R. (ed.), *Elenchus of Biblica* (Rome: Biblical Institute).

Onfray, Michel. *In Defense of Atheism*. Translated by Jeremy Leggatt. London: Serpent's Tail, 2007.

Pasquini, John J. *Atheism and Salvation*. Lanham: University Press of America, 2000.

———. *Ecce Fides*. China: S of C Publications, 2007.

———. *Light, Happiness, and Peace*. New York: 2004.

———. *Pro-Life*. New York: iUniverse, 2003.

———. *Secularism*. New York: Xlibris, 2006.

Perkins, P. *Reading the New Testament*. Second Edition. New York: Paulist Press, 1988.

Phillips, Charles. *Encyclopedia of the Word in Our Time*. New York: McMillan, 2000.

Pinker, Steve. *How the Mind Works*. New York: Norton, 1997.

Price, Simon. *The Oxford Dictionary of Classical Myth and Religion*. Oxford: Oxford University Press, 2004.

Rahner, Karl, and Herbert Vorgrimler. *Theological Dictionary*. Edited by Cornelius Ernst and translated by Richard Stachan. New York: Herder and Herder, 1965.

Rahner, Karl. *Christians at the Crossroads*. Translated by V. Green. New York: The Seabury Press, 1975.

———. *Foundations of Christian Faith: An Introduction to the Idea of Christianity*. Translated by William V. Dych. New York: Crossroads, 1994.

———. *Everyday Faith*. Translated by W.J. O'Hara. New York: Herder and Herder, 1969.

———. *Opportunities for Faith: Elements of a Modern Spirituality*. Translated by Edward Quinn. New York: The Seabury Press, 1978.

———. *Theological Investigations*. Vol. 21, *Science and Christian Faith*. Translated by Hugh M. Riley. New York: Crossroad Publishing Co., 1981.

———. *Theology for Renewal*. Translated Cecily Hastings. New York: Sheed and Ward, 1964.

———. *Encyclopedia of Theology: A Concise Sacramentum Mundi*. New York: Crossroad, 1984.

———. "What Does Vatican II Teach About Atheism?" Translated by Theodore Westow. *Concilium: Theology in the Age of Renewal* 23 (February 1967); 7–24.

Rana, Fazale. *The Cell's Design*. Grand Rapids: BakerBooks, 2008.

Ratzinger, Joseph. *Without Roots*. New York: Basic Books, 2006.

Rawlinson, George. *Ancient History: The Great Civilizations from 3000 B.C. to the Fall of Rome*. New York: Barnes and Nobles, 1993.

Reardon, David. *Aborted Women—Silent No More*. Westchester: Crossway Books, 1987.

Regan, George. *New Trends in Moral Theology*. New York: Newman, 1971.

Reich, Robert. "The Last Word: Bush's God," *The American Prospect* (June 17, 2004).

Reiser, Teri and Paul. *Help for Post-Abortion Woman*. Grand Rapids: Zondervan, 1989.

Reventlow, H. *Problems of Old Testament Theology in the Twentieth Century*. Philadelphia: Fortress, 1985.

Rizzuto, A.M. *The Birth of the Living God*. Chicago: University of Chicago Press, 1979.

Robinson, J. M. (director). *The Nag Hammadi Library in English*. New York: Harper and Row, 1977.

Roper, Anita. *The Anonymous Christian*. Translated by Joseph Donceel. New York: Sheed and Ward, 1966.

Rorty, Richard. *Consequences of Pragmaticism*. Minneapolis: University of Minnesota, 1982.

Rothland, Murray. *An Austrian Perspective on the History of Economic Thought*. Hants: Edward Elgar, 1995.

Runciman, Steven. A History of the Crusades. Vols. 1–3. Cambridge: Cambridge University Press, 1952.

Runes, Dagobert, ed., *Dictionary of Philosophy*. Savage: Littlefield Publishers, Inc., 1983.

Russell, Bertrand. *Religion and Science*. New York: Oxford University Press, 1997.

Ryan, Peter. *Explorers and Mapmakers*. London: Belitha Press, 1939.

Sanchez-Sorondo, Marcelo. *Vitoria*. Washington: Catholic University Press, 1997.

Sanger, Margaret. *The Pivot of Civilization; Birth Control Review; The Woman Rebel; Woman in the New Race;* Swarthmore College Library Edition.

Sartre, Jean Paul. *Existentialism*. Translated by B. Frechtman. New York: Philosophical Library, 1947.

———. *Les Mots*. New York: Braziller, 1964.

Sacra Pagina Series. Collegeville: The Liturgical Press, 2002.

Sacramentum Verbi. Vols. 1–3. New York: Herder and Herder, 1970.

Schmidt, Alvin. *Under the Influence: How Christianity Transformed Civilization*. Grand Rapids: Zondervan, 2001.

Schmidt, Charles. *The Social Results of Early Christianity*. London: Sir Isaac Pitman and Sons, 1907.

Schmidt, W. *The Origin and Growth of Religion*. Second Edition. Translated by H.J. Rose. London: Methuen, 1935.

Scott, James. *The Spanish Origin of International Law*. Washington: Georgetown University Press, 1928.

Schumpeter, Joseph. *History of Economic Analysis*. Oxford: Oxford University Press, 1963.

Scott, John. *A Dictionary of Sociology*. Oxford: Oxford University Press, 2009.

Sidgwick, Henry. *Methods of Ethics*. London: MacMillan, 1907.

Singer, Peter. *Practical Ethics*. Cambridge: University Press, 1993.

Sparks, H.F.D. ed., *The Apocryphal Old Testament*. Oxford: Clarendon, 1984.

Spero, M.H. *Religious Objects as Psychological Structures*. Chicago: University of Chicago Press, 1984.

Spinoza, Benedictus de. *Ethics*. Translated by Edwin Curley. Vol. 1. *The Collected Writings of Spinoza*. Princeton: Princeton University Press, 1985.

———. *Theological-Political Treatise*. Translated by Samuel Shirley. Indianapolis: Hackett Publishing, 2001.

Starkey, Dinah. *Scholastic Atlas of Exploration*. New York: Harper Collins, 1993.

Stevens, Edward. *Making Moral Decisions*. New York: Paulist Press, 1981.

Sulloway, Frank. *Born to Rebel*. New York: Pantheon, 1996.

Tallon, Andrew. "The Anthropological Turn." *The Thomist* 43 (1979): 95–118.

Tierney, Brian. *The Idea of Natural Rights*. Grand Rapids: William Eerdmans, 2001.

Turcan, Robert. *The Cults of the Roman Empire*. Translated by Antonia Nevill. Oxford: Blackwell, 1996.

Udias, Agustin. *Searching the Heavens and the Earth*. Dordrecht: Kluwer Academic Publishers, 2003.

Ulansey, David. *The Origins of the Mithraic Mysteries*. New York: Oxford University Press, 1989.

Ulhorn, Gerhard. *Christian Charity in the Ancient Church*. New York: Charles Scribner's Sons, 1883.

Varghese, Roy. "The Supreme Science." *Viewpoints*. December 16, 2004: 35A.

Vermaseren, Maarten. *Cybele and Attis*. London: Thames and Hudson, 1977.

Vermes, G., *The Dead Sea Scrolls in English*. Third Edition. London: Penguin Press, 1987.

Vitz, Paul. *Faith of the Fatherless: The Psychology of Atheism*. Dallas: Spence, 1999.

Vought, Jeanette. *Post Abortion Trauma*. Grand Rapids: Zondervan, 1991.

Walsh, James. *The Popes and Science*. New York: Fordham University Press, 1911.

Wells, Jonathan. *The Politically Incorrect Guide to Darwinism and Intelligent Design*. Washington: Regnery, 2006.

Wilson, Margaret, ed. *The Essential Descartes*. Translated by Elizabeth Haldane. New York: the New American Library, Inc., 1969.

Wong, David. *Moral Relativity*. Berkeley: University of California Press, 1986.

Woodard, Thomas. *Darwin Strikes Back*. Grand Rapids: Baker Books, 2006.

Woods, Thomas. *How the Catholic Church Built Western Civilization*. Washington: Regnery, 2005.